AUTHORITY
to
HEAL

STUDY GUIDE

STUDY GUIDE

AUTHORITY
to
HEAL

RESTORING THE LOST INHERITANCE OF
God's Healing Power

RANDY CLARK

DESTINY IMAGE® PUBLISHERS, INC.

P.O. Box 310, Shippensburg, PA 17257-0310

"Promoting Inspired Lives."

This book and all other Destiny Image and Destiny Image Fiction books are available at Christian bookstores and distributors worldwide.

Cover design by Eileen Rockwell
Interior design by Terry Clifton

For more information on foreign distributors, call 717-532-3040.

Reach us on the Internet: www.destinyimage.com.

ISBN 13 TP: 978-0-7684-0880-5

For Worldwide Distribution, Printed in the U.S.A.

1 2 3 4 5 6 7 8 / 20 19 18 17 16

SESSIONS

HOW TO USE YOUR STUDY GUIDE

The *Authority to Heal* Study Guide is divided into eight sessions and includes forty days of reinforcement devotionals designed to encourage you to engage in a period of spiritual formation based on the material presented.

Each week, study participants will:

1. Watch a group session. These weekly sessions are designed to be watched in a group or class setting or by a single individual; however, a group setting is highly recommended as it will enable you to maximize the material presented. These sessions will consist of:

   a. Summary of the weekly session.

   b. Discussion questions for group/class/individual discussion and reflection.

   c. Group activation exercise: After watching the session, taking notes, and engaging in discussion, you will take what you have learned and put it to work in the context of your small group or class.

2. Keep up with daily exercises. As you work through the exercises, keep a journal on hand to record your thoughts in response to the reflection questions to stimulate deeper spiritual formation. These daily activities are designed to reinforce the material you learned during the group sessions. They consist of the following:

   a. Devotional reading: Daily devotional segments offer an outlet for increased clarification of the week's topics and provide opportunity for meditation.

   b. Reflection questions: These are designed to help you critically interact with the material you are learning in the sessions.

c. Prayer directive: All ministry starts in the place of prayer. These short, simple prayer topics help you give voice to the empowering work of the Holy Spirit in your life.

MARKED BY HIS POWER

Just as the early disciples received the empowering of the Holy Spirit and ministered powerfully in the name of Jesus, you can too. God is inviting you into the supernatural lifestyle that He intends for all believers.

In the last days, God says, I will pour out my Spirit on all people (Acts 2:17).

SESSION 1 SUMMARY

From the moment you received Jesus as your Lord and Savior, He has been inviting you into a supernatural lifestyle. When you accept His invitation, it will transform the way you understand what the Christian faith looks like and how we are to function as Christians in the world today. God desires to use you, and He makes His Holy Spirit available to equip you for this task. Living a supernatural lifestyle should be normative for all believers, not something unusual that is relegated to a few. Moving in the gifts of healing, in the authority of the name of Jesus, and in the power of the Holy Spirit is one way we carry out the Great Commission. The good news of the gospel of Jesus Christ cannot be advanced through our human endeavors. God's Kingdom advances in His power and authority.

In this session you will have an opportunity to reflect on passages of Scripture that enlighten our understanding of the authority that is available to all believers and to examine what this looks like in your own life. God desires that you and all believers be equipped for the work of ministry so that the Church can operate fully as the empowered body of Jesus Christ in the earth today. So much has been made available to the Church, and we, as believers, should not be willing to settle for less.

DISCUSSION QUESTIONS

1. Read Acts 2. How does the third person of the Trinity—the Holy Spirit—figure in your life?

2. What do you currently believe about the role of the Holy Spirit in the life of the Church and each believer? Why?

3. Why do you think so many Christians don't understand the role of the Holy Spirit in the Christian life?

4. We are living in the time between the book of Acts and the book of Revelation. Are you marked by God's power and authority? What does that statement mean to you?

5. Are you willing to *settle for less* or are you *hungry for more*? Explain.

6. Have willing group/class members briefly share their own experiences of spiritual formation, specifically looking for those who have experienced the power of the Holy Spirit in their life and ministry and how this power and authority has impacted them.

GROUP ACTIVATION EXERCISE

John the Baptist said, "I baptize you with water for repentance. But after me will come one who is more powerful than I, whose sandals I am not fit to carry. He will baptize you with the Holy Spirit and with fire" (Matthew 3:11).

You are invited to embrace the fullness of God's supernatural lifestyle right now, through this prayer for the baptism of the Holy Spirit.

Heavenly Father, I come before you now, thankful that Jesus saved me through His finished work on the cross. I ask that you baptize me now in the Holy Spirit, which I will receive by faith, so that Your power and authority may come upon me, equipping me for Your service. Thank you, Lord Jesus. Amen!

"So Jesus said to them again, "Peace to you! As the Father has sent Me, I also send you." And when He had said this, He breathed on them, and said to them, "Receive the Holy Spirit" (John 20:21-22 NKJV).

WEEKLY READING ASSIGNMENT

Read the Introduction and Chapters 1 and 2 in *Authority to Heal* and be sure to complete your study guide assignments.

SESSION NOTES

DAY ONE

RESTORING THE MANDATE TO HEAL OTHERS

When Jesus' earthly ministry was inaugurated at His baptism in Galilee, all three persons of the Trinity were present. "As soon as *Jesus* was baptized, He went up out of the water. At that moment heaven was opened, and he saw the *Spirit of God* descending like a dove and lighting on Him. And *a voice from heaven* said, "This is my Son, whom I love; with Him I am well pleased" (Matthew 3:16-17).

At His baptism, the Holy Spirit came upon Jesus to equip Him for the divine work set before Him, and immediately He was led into the wilderness by the Spirit, where He established His authority over Satan. Then He commenced His earthly ministry, which consisted of teaching, preaching, and healing, all done in the power and authority of the Spirit.

God's mandate is for all believers to walk in supernatural exploits with Jesus as our model. This supernatural lifestyle is not intended to be peripheral to the gospel, but integral. We are commissioned with a multi-generational commission that will continue until the second coming and is available to whosoever believes in Jesus (see John 14:12-13).

REFLECTION QUESTIONS

1. If God's mandate is for each of us to walk in supernatural exploits with Jesus as our model, how does this truth change the way in which you understand your role in the advance of the Kingdom?

2. In the gospel of Mark, one of the first recorded acts of Jesus is to drive an evil spirit out of a demon-possessed man. In Mark 1:24, the demon, confronted

13

with the presence of Jesus, recognizes Him immediately as the One with all power and authority, and responds accordingly, "What do you want with us, Jesus of Nazareth? Have you come to destroy us? I know who you are—the Holy One of God!"

If you are a believer, this same Jesus lives within you today. In the power of the Holy Spirit, you carry the same authority. Does your theology agree with the identity of Jesus as found in the Scriptures? If not, what do you need to do to bring your theology into alignment with the Word of God?

PRAYER

Heavenly Father, thank You for the provision of your precious Holy Spirit who has come to dwell in us; to be our helper, counselor, and advocate; to empower and equip us; and to remain with us until the end of the age. Thank You that your Spirit guides us in all truth, comforts us in our affliction, and through Him we are able to bear fruit for your Kingdom. Give us a fuller vision of the Holy Spirit in our lives so that we may bring glory to You in thought, word, and deed.

JESUS COMMISSIONED ALL BELIEVERS TO HEAL THE SICK

In Jesus' farewell discourse to His disciples, He emphasizes that He is a full revelation of the Father, using the miracles He performed as evidence. "Believe me when I say that I am in the Father and the Father is in me; or at least believe on the evidence of the miracles themselves" (John 14:11). Then, Jesus lays the groundwork for the disciples to understand that they will be able to continue the work of advancing the Kingdom of God on the earth that He (Jesus) began. "I tell you the truth, anyone who has faith in me will do what I have been doing. He will do even greater things than these, because I am going to the Father" (John 14:12). These "greater things" are miracles that believers will do in the power and authority of the Holy Spirit, whom Jesus will send once He has ascended. Jesus then finishes this teaching by assuring His disciples that they will be able to carry forward the work He began, because He [Jesus Himself] will answer their prayers when they are prayed in accordance with His will. "And I will do whatever you ask in my name, so that the Son may bring glory to the Father. You may ask me for anything in my name, and I will do it" (John 14:13-14).

Nowhere in the Scriptures do we hear Jesus or the apostles teaching that the gifts of healings and miracles will cease. But along the way in the history of the Church, inadequate biblical discipleship based on wrong theology stripped away the knowledge of the power and authority of God to heal and of His desire to heal. The good news of the gospel became separated from the power and authority of all believers. We lost our spiritual inheritance—our birthright from Jesus' finished work of the cross. Tradition began to negate the commands of God.

REFLECTION QUESTIONS

1. Read Matthew 28:16–20. What is Jesus' mandate in this passage, and what are His follow-up instructions? What is your understanding of the concepts presented by Jesus in this passage in the context of the twenty-first century Church?

2. John 14:12-13 says that *anyone who has faith in Jesus* is included in this multigenerational commission. Assuming you have faith in Jesus, *anyone* includes you; therefore, you have the power and authority to advance God's Kingdom here on the earth through the Holy Spirit. How does this truth resonate with you as a believer with a mandate to carry out the Great Commission?

PRAYER

Gracious and loving heavenly Father, we hear Your voice and yield our lives to You. Come and accomplish a mighty work in us. Open the eyes of our heart so that we may see you in the light of your glory. Pour out your spirit on us so that we may be participants rather than spectators, bearing testimony to the power of Your faithfulness as we help hasten the coming of Your Kingdom.

THE KINGDOM OF GOD

In Chapter 1, Randy shares candidly how his childhood was profoundly shaped by experiences of God's healing. The miracle-working power and authority of God was not merely a theoretical concept in his life, but a real experience. Likewise, the Church, beginning in the book of Acts, has been profoundly shaped by experiences of God's mighty power and authority, although you will not always find this truth taught in seminaries and Bible colleges. As Jesus said in Mark 7:8, "You [we] have let go of the commands of God and are holding on to the traditions of men." We must not continue to make the mistake of neglecting the miraculous, thereby denying Jesus the glory He deserves.

In the story of Saul's conversion, God uses an ordinary believer, a man named Ananias, to minister healing to Saul's eyes and to baptize him (Saul) in the Holy Spirit. We know that after his conversion, Saul became the apostle Paul who brought the gospel to the Gentiles and became one of the most significant figures in Christianity. God is still in the business of using ordinary believers like Ananias and you and me to advance His Kingdom on the earth today. But in order for God's power and authority to be restored to the Church, we must dismantle the widespread expectation of unbelief that has too long replaced an expectation for the miraculous in the life of believers, and it begins in each one of us.

REFLECTION QUESTIONS

1. As we can see from Randy's personal story, a willingness to embrace the supernatural aspect of God so often comes from personal experience with the power and authority of God. What is your personal experience with the power and authority of God?

2. In Mark 7:8–23, Jesus is addressing the hypocrisy and spiritually bankrupt state of the Pharisees, who are holding on to the traditions of men while letting go of the commands of God. While most of us are thankfully not in the poor spiritual condition of the Pharisees Jesus was addressing, nonetheless we are too often guilty of cleaving to religious tradition at the expense of the commands of God. How true is this in your own life?

PRAYER

O Lord, we come with repentant hearts. Forgive our unproductiveness and create in us a radical new beginning so that we might receive Your covenant blessings as we remember the words of Hosea 10:12: "Sow for yourselves righteousness, reap the fruit of unfailing love, and break up your unplowed ground; for it is time to seek the Lord, until He comes and showers righteousness on you."

EXPECTATION AND THE MIRACULOUS

When Jesus walked the earth, those who were in need of a miracle expected something from Him, and as a result they approached Him from a posture of expectation. Jesus carried an authority that generated expectation. The men who lowered their friend through the roof in order to get him in front of Jesus were most certainly expecting a miracle from Jesus. The centurion who approached Jesus on the road and asked Him to "just say the word, and my servant will be healed" obviously came with knowledge of Jesus' authority and an expectation of His power.

Sadly, much of the Church has lost its expectation for the miraculous, forgetting the authority of Jesus that is available to all believers. The early faith community understood their role as conduits through whom the Spirit of God could freely flow, but over time we allowed our role to be shaped by the hearts of men rather than the will of God. In one of his sermons, A.W. Tozer put it this way: "If the Holy Spirit was withdrawn from the church today, 95 percent of what we do would go on and no one would know the difference. If the Holy Spirit had been withdrawn from the New Testament church, 95 percent of what they did would stop, and everybody would know the difference."

REFLECTION QUESTIONS

1. Throughout the world today there are still those believers who operate in the ministry of deliverance, setting people free from the bonds of Satan through the power and authority of the Holy Spirit. If the demons they expel understand the authority of Jesus and the power that is His, why do we not also understand this truth?

2. Based on Revelation 19:10, "For the testimony of Jesus is the spirit of prophecy," how would you explain the connection between expectation and the miraculous?

PRAYER

Dear Jesus, forgive us for continually forgetting that You gave everything for us while we give so little to You. Make us courageous, so that we might lay your firm foundation for those who come behind us. Equip us and strengthen us through the Holy Spirit until we fully become your people, ready to do Your will.

CALLING FORTH THE ANOINTED BODY OF CHRIST

The apostle Paul, in his letter to the church in Colossae, sets forth the supremacy of Christ and His (Jesus') headship over the Church. "And He is the head of the body, the church; He is the beginning and the firstborn from among the dead, so that in everything He might have the supremacy" (Col. 1:18). In his letter to the Ephesians, Paul tells us that we are "members of His body" (Eph. 5:30), and that it is God's intention that each one of us attains the whole measure of the fullness of Christ (see Eph. 4:13). We do this through unity in the faith and knowledge of Jesus, which leads to maturity. God desires we become "mature" believers in order that we are not tossed about by every teaching of men. He wants us to be grounded in His truths so that we can "grow up into him who is the Head, that is, Christ" (Eph. 4:15).

We are the anointed body of Christ and it is vital we understand this truth. God intends for us, the Church, to operate fully as the empowered body of Jesus in the earth today, and in order for this to be accomplished we must be activated in the gifts and anointing of the Holy Spirit. We must return to a dependency upon the person and work of the Holy Spirit if we are to see the power ministry of Jesus continue in our time and beyond.

REFLECTIVE QUESTIONS

1. As a member of the body of Christ, how are you allowing God to prepare you for works of service?

2. What does it mean to you to "attain the whole measure of the fullness of Christ"?

PRAYER

Father, thank you for the magnificent inheritance you have given us in Christ Jesus. May we submit to having the eyes of our hearts enlightened by your Holy Spirit so that we may know what is the hope to which you are calling us and embrace the riches of our glorious inheritance.

FOUNDATIONS FOR DIVINE HEALING

We need look no further than the Bible to see the biblical basis for the continuation of spiritual gifts, but in order to do so many must make their way past the confusion created by the enemy of our souls who labors tirelessly to keep the Church as powerless as possible.

And as you go, preach, saying, "The kingdom of heaven is at hand." Heal the sick, cleanse the lepers, raise the dead, cast out demons. Freely you have received, freely give (Matthew 10:7-8 NKJV).

SESSION 2 SUMMARY

Healing flows from the very nature of God. Yahweh-Rophe healed through Moses and many of His prophets, who were "types" of Jesus, the Messiah who was to come. Jesus brought the in-break of the Kingdom of God with its healing power, commissioning all believers to heal the sick. The old and new covenants, the atoning work of Christ on the cross, and the in-break of the Kingdom of God combine to form the basis for divine healing in the life of the Church.

The enemy has vehemently opposed the contemporary relevance of the gifts of the Spirit necessary for divine healing by throwing many confusing philosophies that are not of God against this truth. In order for the Church, as a whole, to see the ministry of healing restored, there must be a biblical return to the availability and authority of the supernatural, which includes a theology of healing demonstration and empowerment. God, in His sovereignty, has decided to impart the Holy Spirit to His people and use them as conduits to release His power in the earth. It is not a matter of whether or not He wants to heal. God still heals and He wants to heal through you and me. We must learn how to be His conduits. For spiritual gifts to be released and activated in the Church today, we must return to the "elementary teaching" of impartation. God has promised another final and radical outpouring among the nations before His Son returns. Again, He will bring it about through His people. Jesus said, "As the Father has sent me, I am sending you" (John 20:21).

DISCUSSION QUESTIONS

1.   In Exodus 15:26 God reveals himself to His people using the name Yahweh-Rophe, which means "the God who heals." Why do you think healing is so central to the heart of God?

2.   Read Hebrews 8:6. The writer of Hebrews says that the New Covenant is "founded on better promises." Among these better promises we find Romans 8:2–4, which says that through the work of the cross, God's laws now live in our hearts, not on stone tablets, so that—empowered by the Spirit—we can delight in doing God's will. How do you think God intends this New Covenant promise to reflect His nature in the Church today?

3.   In First Corinthians 2:1–5 Paul is exhorting the church in Corinth to not look to the eloquence or intellectual prowess of man as a revelation of God, but to understand that it is in the demonstration of His power that God reveals Himself. Why do you think God uses demonstrations of His power to reveal Himself instead of just words?

4.   The New Testament standard for discipleship, as revealed in the parables of Jesus, indicates that the Kingdom of God will inaugurate with power and great growth. If Jesus inaugurated His Kingdom with power and pronounced that it is to experience great growth, how does that translate into the powerless Church we see today?

5.   Jesus, God in the flesh, demonstrated great humility during His time on earth, always giving glory to His Father rather than taking it for Himself. We are called to the same humility as ministers of the gospel, but why is humility so often "easier said than done" when it comes to the ministry of healing?

6.   Read Acts 19:13–20, the story of some who falsely attempted to heal in the name of Jesus. Who in this story understood the sons of Sceva to be false healers, what was the end result of this whole episode, and why is this important for us to know?

7. Chapter 6 of *Authority to Heal* clearly lays out the theological foundations for impartation, yet the Church today seems to have lost this elementary teaching that was given to us as found in Hebrews 6:1–3. Why is impartation necessary for the advance of the Kingdom?

GROUP ACTIVATION EXERCISE

Break up into small groups of two or three. Using Discussion Question #2, reflect on what it means in your life to delight in doing God's will and reflect His nature in both the Church and the world today.

WEEKLY READING ASSIGNMENT

Read Chapters 3–6 in *Authority to Heal*, and be sure to complete your study guide assignments.

SESSION NOTES

THE NATURE OF GOD

For God so loved the world that He gave His one and only Son, that whoever believes in him shall not perish but have eternal life (John 3:16).

Because healing flows from the very nature of God, the Church Jesus died to establish should reflect God's nature. It should come as no surprise that one of the most significant ways in which Satan has succeeded in rendering the Church powerless over the centuries has been to cause us to cease being a full reflection of the nature of God by turning us away from a supernatural lifestyle. Through a twisting of doctrine, theologies have arisen that convinced us that the charismata—the spiritual gifts—are no longer needed or available to believers. This is simply not true, and it is important that we understand that Satan does not deal in truth. Every page of the gospels reflects the authority and power of Jesus and the nature of God.

Love is such a foundational part of God's nature. His ultimate act of love is expressed in Jesus. Jesus is the living Word, the logos, embodying God's divine reason and creative order and His great love.

REFLECTION AND QUESTIONS

In order to reflect the love of God, we need to receive His love—we need to fall in love with our Creator. Today I invite you to spend quiet time reflecting on the Lord's Prayer from Matthew 6:9–13.

This, then, is how you should pray: "Our Father in heaven, hallowed be your name, your kingdom come, your will be done on earth as it is in heaven. Give us today our daily bread. Forgive us our debts, as we also have forgiven our debtors. And lead us not into temptation, but deliver us from the evil one."

1. There are six aspects of God's nature revealed in the Lord's Prayer. As Jesus prays to His Father He reveals that God the Father is present and with us, He is holy and pure, powerful with all authority, our provider, the One who pardons our transgressions, and protects us from the evil one. How do you see God's nature reflected in your life?

2. Are there any aspects of God's nature that are preventing you from falling in love with Him? If so, what are they and where did your understanding of them come from?

3. The apostle Paul says, "The life I live in the body, I live by faith in the Son of God, who loved me and gave himself for me" (Gal. 2:20). Reflect on how you personally fathom such love as demonstrated by God in Jesus.

PRAYER DIRECTIVE

Ask the Holy Spirit to give you a revelation of the Father's heart so that you might begin to explore the depths of His great love. If we are to receive and properly steward God's spiritual gifts, we must first understand His great love.

Father, we rejoice in the knowledge that you have present and future blessings for us that are beyond our imagination. Our hearts delight in You! We invite You to build Your Kingdom in our hearts today.

CONTINUATION OF SPIRITUAL GIFTS

*All authority in heaven and on earth has been given to me. Therefore
go and make disciples of all nations, baptizing them in the name of
the Father and of the Son and of the Holy Spirit, and teaching them
to obey everything I have commanded you. And surely I am with
you always, to the very end of the age* (Matthew 28:18–20).

After His crucifixion, Jesus' body is prepared for burial and placed in a tomb with a large rock sealing the entrance and guards posted outside. After the Sabbath, the women return to the tomb to complete the preparation of the body, only to find the tomb empty. "The one you seek is no longer buried there. He has risen," says the angel. And so it begins—Jesus' disciples struggle to understand that their beloved Lord has risen from the grave.

Remembering that Jesus told them to go to a mountain in Galilee, the disciples go and assemble there, and just as He said He would Jesus appears to them, commissioning them to carry on the work that He did during His time on earth.

"All authority has been given to me," He says. "Therefore go and make disciples...baptizing...and teaching them to obey everything I have commanded you." This commission is the New Testament standard for discipleship. We are to baptize those who are new to the faith and then disciple them to do what Jesus taught His disciples to do—heal the sick and cast out demons. This is a perpetual commission, not a one-time directive, and it carries a promise from Jesus that He will be with us in this that He has tasked us with until the end of the age when He returns. In other words, the same power and authority that enabled Jesus' ministry is available to enable us today.

REFLECTION AND QUESTIONS

Five-fold Office Gifts of Jesus

Spend time today reflecting on Paul's teaching on the five-fold office gifts of Christ found in Ephesians.

> But to each one of us grace has been given as Christ apportioned it. This is why it says: "When He ascended on high, He led captives in His train and gave gifts to men." (What does "He ascended" mean except that He also descended to the lower, earthly regions? He who descended is the very one who ascended higher than all the heavens, in order to fill the whole universe.) It was He who gave some to be apostles, some to be prophets, some to be evangelists, and some to be pastors and teachers, to prepare God's people for works of service, so that the body of Christ may be built up until we all reach unity in the faith and in the knowledge of the Son of God and become mature, attaining to the whole measure of the fullness of Christ (Ephesians 4:7–13).

1. Notice that it says that we are to exercise these gifts to "prepare God's people for works of service, so that the body of Christ may be built up until we all reach unity...attaining to the whole measure of the fullness of Christ." This is an ongoing process and we are each called to participate. How has Christ called you to participate in this process?

Fruits of Righteousness for the Children of God

Read John 15:1–17 and Philippians 1:9-10, reflecting on the connection between fruits of the spirit and the glory of God.

> I am the true vine, and my Father is the gardener. He cuts off every branch in me that bears no fruit, while every branch that does bear fruit He prunes so that it will be even more fruitful. You are already clean because of the word I have spoken to you. Remain in me, and I will remain in you. No branch can bear fruit by itself; it must remain in the vine. Neither can you bear fruit unless you remain in me. I am the vine; you are the branches. If a man remains in me and I in him, he will bear much fruit; apart from me you can do nothing. If anyone does not remain in me, he is like a branch that is thrown away and withers; such branches are picked up, thrown into the fire and burned. If you remain in me and my words remain in you, ask whatever you wish, and it will be given you. This is to my Father's glory, that you bear much fruit, showing yourselves to be my disciples (John 15:1–8).

And this is my prayer: that your love may abound more and more in knowledge and depth of insight, so that you may be able to discern what is best and may be pure and blameless until the day of Christ, filled with the fruit of righteousness that comes through Jesus Christ—to the glory and praise of God (Philippians 1:9–11).

2. The fruit of John 15 reveals the inner working of the Spirit that makes us fruitful. This work of the Spirit is grounded in love and opens up to more and more "knowledge and depth of insight," as Paul references in the Philippians passage. In turn, this knowledge and insight reveal the purposes of God, enabling us to pray confidently. Confident prayers are powerful prayers that manifest miracles and healings. How has God pruned you? What was the result of His pruning?

PRAYER

Dear Lord, equip us and strengthen us for the tasks before us, that we might be Your people. Create in us willing hearts, ready to do Your will. Give us courage to ask boldly in Your name, believing your promises, that we might by your grace reap a rich harvest for Your Kingdom here on earth.

Sow for yourselves righteousness, reap the fruit of unfailing love, and break up your unplowed ground; for it is time to seek the Lord, until He comes and showers righteousness on you (Hosea 10:12).

MYSTERY OF DIVINE HEALING

Whereby are given unto us exceeding great and precious promises: that by these ye might be partakers of the divine nature (2 Peter 1:4 KJV).

As we read through the gospels, we see Jesus moving in power and authority, teaching, preaching, healing, and ministering deliverance. He is God in the flesh, bringing the Kingdom of God to bear on a lost and broken world, and He operates with the confidence and authority of one who knows His heavenly Father intimately. And then we come to Mark 6:1–6 where the power and authority of Jesus seems to be at a low ebb. Further along in the New Testament we find the apostle Paul operating powerfully in the gifts of the Spirit. So strong was the anointing on Paul that people would take the cloths he wore around his head as he worked and be healed just from touching them. And yet, like Jesus, we find Paul's anointing at low ebb from time to time (see 2 Tim. 4:20; Gal. 4:13; and Phil. 2:25-27).

We know that Jesus chose to live dependent upon the anointing of the Holy Spirit to release divine healing ("the power of the Lord was present for him to heal the sick," Luke 5:17), and yet His power ebbed and flowed, not because power and authority were not available, but because of the lack of faith present in those around Him (in His hometown). Just as Jesus and His disciples in the early Church experienced periods of ebb and flow as they ministered, so will we today experience the same ebb and flow. We know that God chooses to minister healing through human vessels, and yet there remains a great deal of mystery associated with the ministry of divine healing. When we minister, we can never predict who will be healed. God is sovereign and we will not always understand His ways.

REFLECTION AND QUESTIONS

Read and reflect on Matthew 17:14–21, and Mark 9:14–29.

When they came to the crowd, a man approached Jesus and knelt before him. "Lord, have mercy on my son," he said. "He has seizures and is suffering greatly. He often falls into the fire or into the water. I brought him to your disciples, but they could not heal him." "O unbelieving and perverse generation," Jesus replied, "how long shall I stay with you? How long shall I put up with you? Bring the boy here to me." Jesus rebuked the demon, and it came out of the boy, and he was healed from that moment. Then the disciples came to Jesus in private and asked, "Why couldn't we drive it out?" He replied, "Because you have so little faith. I tell you the truth, if you have faith as small as a mustard seed, you can say to this mountain, 'Move from here to there' and it will move. Nothing will be impossible for you" (Matthew 17:14–21).

After Jesus had gone indoors, His disciples asked him privately, "Why couldn't we drive it out?" He replied, "This kind can come out only by prayer" (Mark 9:28-29).

1. We must approach the ministry from a posture of humility, always recognizing that the authority to heal the sick comes exclusively through the supreme name of Jesus Christ, who is perfect theology. The anointing and authority to heal the sick has nothing to do with us and everything to do with Jesus, who works through us. Have you experienced the ebb of God's power and authority while ministering, and, if so, how did you respond?

2. In Mark 9:28-29 Jesus tells His disciples how to respond when healing doesn't come—they are to pray and fast. He is not giving them a one-time fix but rather inviting them into a lifestyle. If you minister to someone and they are not healed, why is this not God's deficiency?

PRAYER

Dear Father, increase our faith in facing the challenges of today until it bursts forth in action that honors you and accomplishes your will. Sustain us when we are weary, protect us from discouragement, and empower us to believe, knowing your grace is sufficient for us. Give us the will to follow in faith where you lead.

"My grace is sufficient for you, for my power is made perfect in weakness." Therefore I will boast all the more gladly about my weaknesses, so that Christ's power may rest on me (2 Corinthians 12:9).

MOTIVATION FOR DIVINE HEALING

If anyone speaks, he should do it as one speaking the very words of God.
If anyone serves, he should do it with the strength God provides, so
that in all things God may be praised through Jesus Christ. To him be
the glory and the power for ever and ever. Amen (1 Peter 4:11).

It is the night before Jesus' crucifixion. He and His disciples have gathered in an upper room to share a meal. As they recline at the table together Jesus begins to share some of His last words with those closest to Him. He begins by comforting them, telling them He is the way to the Father and that He will send the precious Holy Spirit to empower them and lead them in all truth. Then He uses the analogy of the vine and the branches to illustrate how there is no fruitfulness apart from fellowship with Him. "If you remain in me and my words remain in you, ask whatever you wish, and it will be given you. This is to my Father's glory, that you bear much fruit, showing yourselves to be my disciples" (John 15:7-8).

Within this passage lies the motivation for all divine healing—to give God glory. Within Scripture we can find many motivations for healing—for the Church to grow, for many to come to Christ, for God's mercy to be revealed, for the love of God to be manifested—but the highest, most pure and unselfish motivation for healing and miracles is so that Jesus' name will be held in high honor and God will be glorified. Jesus' actions were always directed toward glorifying God, and because Jesus is our model we should not settle for less.

REFLECTION AND QUESTIONS

Read Second Thessalonians 1:11-12 and reflect on Paul's words to the Church:

To this end also we pray for you always, that our God will count you worthy of your calling, and fulfill every desire for goodness and the work of faith with power, so that the name of our Lord Jesus will be glorified in you, and you in Him, according to the grace of our God and the Lord Jesus Christ (NASB).

Paul's exhortation to the church in Thessalonica should encourage us today, just as it did those in the early Church, as we stand ready to be counted worthy of our calling—fulfilling every desire for goodness and the work of faith with power—so that the name of Jesus will be glorified in us, remembering that it is God who initiates our every act of faith in His name.

1. If someone were to ask you what it looks like in your life to "fulfill every desire for goodness and the work of faith with power" so that the name of Jesus will be glorified in you, how would you respond?

You alone are the Lord. You made the heavens, even the highest heavens, and all their starry host, the earth and all that is on it, the seas and all that is in them. You give life to everything, and the multitudes of heaven worship you (Nehemiah 9:6).

2. All of creation exists to reveal God's glory. You are the crown of God's creation, made in His image. How does your life reflect His glory?

PRAYER

O Father, let us remember the words of the prophet Isaiah as we draw water with rejoicing from the wells of salvation, giving thanks to You as we call on Your name, making your deeds known among the nations, and proclaiming that Your name be exalted! May we sing for joy of the glorious things you have done so that all the world may hear and know that you alone are Holy (see Isa. 12:3–6).

THE LAYING ON OF HANDS

"Now, Lord, consider their threats and enable your servants to speak your word with great boldness. Stretch out your hand to heal and perform miraculous signs and wonders through the name of your holy servant Jesus." After they prayed, the place where they were meeting was shaken. And they were all filled with the Holy Spirit and spoke the word of God boldly (Acts 4:29–31).

The act of one person imparting the anointing of God to another is biblical and found in both the Old and New Testaments. In the book of John, Jesus appears to His disciples after the resurrection, surprising and frightening them as He comes to stand among them as they huddle in a locked room. Seeing their fear, He says, "'Peace be with you! As the Father has sent me, I am sending you.' And with that He breathed on them and said, 'Receive the Holy Spirit'" (John 20:21-22). In a brief moment in time, these fearful men received the promised gift of the Holy Spirit to empower them for ministry. They will no longer walk alongside the earthly Jesus. Now, with one act of impartation, Jesus lives within them in the power of the Holy Spirit.

In other places in Scripture we find impartation—the transference of anointing—taking place through the laying on of hands. The act of impartation we see in the early Church continued down through the centuries right up to the present time, where it continues to empower the Church today. God intends that this strong biblical concept be an integral part of the life of every believer, so that we are enabled to advance the Kingdom with great boldness, stretching out our hands "to heal and perform miraculous signs and wonders through the name of your holy servant Jesus."

REFLECTION AND QUESTIONS

Read Second Kings 2:9–15, reflecting on this Old Testament account of impartation in which Elijah's anointing is transferred to his spiritual son, Elisha. Notice that what takes place here is a transference of the power of the Spirit of God, not the power of Elijah's human spirit. Likewise, when the people remark that the spirit of Elijah is resting on Elisha, what they are seeing in the Spirit of God working through Elisha, similar to what they had seen in Elijah.

When they had crossed, Elijah said to Elisha, "Tell me, what can I do for you before I am taken from you?" "Let me inherit a double portion of your spirit," Elisha replied. "You have asked a difficult thing," Elijah said, "yet if you see me when I am taken from you, it will be yours—otherwise not." As they were walking along and talking together, suddenly a chariot of fire and horses of fire appeared and separated the two of them, and Elijah went up to heaven in a whirlwind. Elisha saw this and cried out, "My father! My father! The chariots and horsemen of Israel!" And Elisha saw him no more. Then he took hold of his own clothes and torn them apart. He picked up the cloak that had fallen from Elijah and went back and stood on the bank of the Jordan. Then he took the cloak that had fallen from him and struck the water with it. "Where now is the Lord, the God of Elijah?" he asked. When he struck the water, it divided to the right and to the left, and he crossed over. The company of the prophets from Jericho, who were watching, said, "The spirit of Elijah is resting on Elisha." And they went to meet him and bowed to the ground before him (2 Kings 2:9–15).

1. What is your impression of what happens to a person when they receive an impartation?

Read Second Timothy 1:6-7, reflecting on Paul's exhortation to Timothy encouraging him to be faithful and to use the gifts of the Spirit that Paul himself imparted to Timothy.

For this reason I remind you fan into flame the gift of God, which is in you through the laying on of my hands. For God did not give us a spirit of timidity, but a spirit of power, of love and of self-discipline.

2. How does your heart respond to the gift of impartation God has for you?

PRAYER DIRECTIVE

You may have received an impartation in the past, but God always has more for you. If you feel a stirring in your heart for more of the authority of God in your life, ask the Lord to impart His Holy Spirit to you now.

Lord, create a hunger in me now for the "more" of impartation of your Spirit and your gifts. Create faith in me now to receive gifts through impartation, to receive a new and possibly stronger "filling" of Your Spirit through an impartation. I ask this in the power and authority of Jesus' name. Amen.

THE ISSUE OF FAITH IN HEALING

God's faith comes from God's grace, and for us this grace is dependent upon a relationship with Jesus—abiding in Him. The nature of faith can seem complex, but the mandate to heal is straightforward. God is intentional about healing, and He is calling us to partner with Him with the same intentionality.

Then the disciples came to Jesus in private and asked, "Why couldn't we drive it out?" He replied, "Because you have so little faith. I tell you the truth, if you have faith as small as a mustard seed, you can say to this mountain, 'Move from here to there' and it will move. Nothing will be impossible for you" (Matthew 17:19–21).

SESSION 3 SUMMARY

In order to learn how to flow in God's supernatural power and authority, we must understand the nature of faith. Although faith is the key and primary way healing is received and demonstrated, God is sovereign and able to perform miracles outside of our confines. We must have faith *of* God in order to take hold of—*seize*—the faith that comes from Him through divine revelation. Our faith can be small but powerful when we believe and receive what God makes available by His grace. God's divine enablement will empower us for the miraculous, coming to us as a situational gift from Him for the moment.

There is a strong connection between healing and faith and the revelatory gifts such as declarations, words of knowledge, prophecy, and teaching. In the same way, there is also a strong connection between hearing and receiving revelation from God that results in faith. All of these revelatory gifts flow out of relationship with Jesus. They are unmerited and happen more often to those who expect them and know how to recognize them. When we teach, especially through testimony, we are laying a foundation that will build faith and an expectation for healing. Our understanding of the nature of faith will enable us to better partner with God in the ministry of healing.

God is intentional about healing, and He will act in ways that express His intentionality. When we learn His ways and study His mighty deeds as found in the Scriptures, we become intimate with Him and are better able to understand what it means to reveal His glory in the ministry of healing. "The promises of God are not a problem to be achieved, but a promise to be received" (Leif Hetland). When we learn to cooperate with the presence of God, ministry moves from laboring and striving to a place of rest and favor.

DISCUSSION QUESTIONS

1.   What is the difference between faith *in* God and faith *of* God, and how does this distinction impact the way in which you understand the nature of faith in terms of operating in the miraculous?

2.   What are some of the ways in which we can receive divine revelation? How do you receive divine revelation?

3.   How can our faith be small and yet be "mountain-moving faith"?

4.   What does it mean to have God's divine enablement empower us as a situational gift for the moment? Have you experienced this?

5.   How do you personally recognize revelatory gifts?

6.   Revelation 19:10 says that the testimony of Jesus is the spirit of prophecy. What do you understand this verse to mean and why is it important to healing ministry?

7.   How do we cooperate with the presence of God in ministry? Share examples from your own ministry times.

GROUP ACTIVATION EXERCISES

To one there is given through the Spirit the message of wisdom, to another the message of knowledge by means of the same Spirit (1 Corinthians 12:8).

Set aside an hour of time for your entire group to meet together. Open in prayer, asking the Lord for words of knowledge. Give everyone about five minutes, encouraging people to write down what they are hearing from God. Invite those who have received words of knowledge to share one of the words they have received. As each person shares, invite those who believe that particular word is for them to stand, and when all words have been given invite those standing to come to the person who spoke that particular word and receive prayer. Allow ample time for prayer. When everyone who wants it has received prayer, invite people to share what God is doing as a result of the word of knowledge and prayer they received.

WEEKLY READING ASSIGNMENT

Reach Chapters 7 and 8 in *Authority to Heal*, and be sure to complete your study guide assignments.

SESSION NOTES

LEARNING TO WALK WITH GOD, BY FAITH

The Lord had said to Abram, "Leave your country, your people and your father's household and go to the land I will show you.
...So Abram left, as the Lord had told him (Genesis 12:1,4).

After this, the word of the Lord came to Abram in a vision: "Do not be afraid, Abram. I am your shield, your very great reward." ...Abram believed the Lord, and He credited it to him as righteousness (Genesis 15:1,6).

But Sarah saw that the son whom Hagar the Egyptian had borne to Abraham was mocking, and she said to Abraham, "Get rid of that slave woman and her son, for that slave woman's son will never share in the inheritance with my son Isaac." The matter distressed Abraham greatly because it concerned his son. But God said to him, "Do not be so distressed about the boy and your maidservant. Listen to whatever Sarah tells you, because it is through Isaac that your offspring will be reckoned (Genesis 21:9–12).

Abraham's story in Genesis 12–25 reveals a pattern of faith that sets an example for all believers. As you read through the story of Abraham in the Genesis narrative you will see a pattern of behavior from Abraham—he hears God's voice, believes what he is hearing, and obeys God on faith. This narrative also reveals Abraham's humanness. Like us, his faith sometimes faltered as he learned how to walk with God. At times, Abraham took matters into his own hands rather than trusting God and bore the consequences in the midst of God's compassion and mercy. If this sounds familiar—not because you know the story of Abraham, but because it resembles your walk of faith—take heart. Learning to live by faith is a process, and God is a patient and compassionate teacher: "The Lord is compassionate and gracious, slow to anger, abounding in love" (Ps. 103:8).

As you press into the issue of faith in healing, remember the words of the writer of Hebrews: "And without faith it is impossible to please God, because anyone who comes to him must believe that He exists and that He rewards those who earnestly seek him" (Heb. 11:6). Jesus wants us to take hold of or seize the faith of God that comes from Him as a gift to us. When we do, He will meet us at that place of faith and bring about His will in our situation. In this way, He advances the Kingdom of God in us and through us.

REFLECTION AND QUESTIONS

Then the Lord said, "I will surely return to you about this time next year, and Sarah your wife will have a son." …Abraham and Sarah were already old and well advanced in years, and Sarah was past the age of childbearing. So Sarah laughed to herself as she thought, "After I am worn out and my master is old, will I now have this pleasure?" (Genesis 18:10–12)

1. Read Genesis 12–25, reflecting on Abraham's pattern of faith in light of your own life. All of us are faced with a myriad of decisions every day, large and small. When it comes to the big decisions in your life, how do you go about making your decisions, and how much do you involve God in the process?

2. Even though God told Sarah and Abraham that they would give birth to a son, instead of trusting God in faith, Sarah did not believe Him. Later, you recall that she took matters into her own hands, giving her maidservant to Abraham in order to produce a son. Lacking faith, Sarah stepped outside of God's plan with disastrous consequences. Are there instances in your life where you have stepped outside of God's plan for you, and if so what were the results?

3. Why is learning to walk in faith important for those called to the ministry of healing?

PRAYER DIRECTIVE

Using the words of Hebrews 12:1–3, ask God to help you persevere, with faith.

Dear Father, help me to run with perseverance the race marked out for me, throwing off everything that hinders me, and the sin that so easily entangles me, fixing my eyes instead on Jesus, the author and perfecter of my faith. For He is the One who endured the cross for the joy set before Him, scorning its shame to sit down at the right hand of Your throne. May I well consider Jesus, the One who endured such opposition from sinful men, so that I do not grow weary and lose heart.

MOUNTAIN-MOVING FAITH

"Have faith in God," Jesus answered. "I tell you the truth, if anyone says to this mountain, 'Go, throw yourself into the sea,' and does not doubt in his heart but believes that what he says will happen, it will be done for him. Therefore I tell you, whatever you ask for in prayer, believe that you have received it, and it will be yours" (Mark 11:22–24).

This passage in Matthew is one of three key passages in Scripture that mention mountain-moving faith. The other passages are Matthew 21:21-22 and Matthew 17:20. Mountain-moving faith as Jesus defines it in the gospels is a manifestation of a grace gift of faith that comes from God the Holy Spirit. All of us at one time or another face "mountains" in our life which need to be moved. We can either try to move then on our own, or we can turn to God in faith and let Him show us how to move them. We will most likely try both methods, because sometimes our faith is stronger than at other times.

Yet even when we trust God in faith to move a mountain in our life, it doesn't always get moved in the way we want or as far as we want. God's ways are not our ways and His thoughts are not our thoughts. We will not always understand what He is doing or why, and that is where the issue of faith must lead us on. Abraham and Sarah could not understand how they could bear a son in their old age. Sarah's faith in God faltered and she tried to move a mountain in her own strength and failed, and yet God still brought about His purposes through Sarah. God's total sufficiency is revealed in our insufficiency.

REFLECTIONS

Using the three passages in the gospels about mountain-moving faith, explore what it looks like in your life to believe that whatever you ask in prayer will happen when you ask in faith. Write down your thoughts.

Has there been an instance when you trusted God in faith that a mountain in your life would be moved and it has not yet happened? How are you processing this?

PRAYER

Dear Jesus, give me the will to follow in faith where You have led the way. May Your mountain-moving faith take hold in my life, so that I may rise up and meet the challenges that threaten to overwhelm me.

Lord, you have assigned me my portion and my cup; you have made my lot secure. The boundary lines have fallen for me in pleasant places; surely I have a delightful inheritance (Psalm 16:5-6).

LOVE, THE MORE EXCELLENT WAY

Now I will show you the most excellent way. If I speak in the tongues of men and of angels, but have not love, I am only a resounding gong or a clanging cymbal. …Love is patient, love is kind. It does not envy, it does not boast, it is not proud. It is not rude, it is not self-seeking, it is not easily angered, it keeps no record of wrongs. Love does not delight in evil but rejoices with the truth. It always protects, always trusts, always hopes, always perseveres. Love never fails (1 Corinthians 12:31; 13:1,4–8).

The stunning "love passage" in First Corinthians 13 is exceedingly well known and exceedingly difficult to live out. Try as we might, we are not always patient or kind. We are sometimes given over to envy and boasting and pride. Who among us has never been rude or self-seeking or angry? And how often do we keep a list of wrongs to justify our actions? Even though we do not delight in evil and rejoice with the truth, many of us are a far cry from being apostles of love. And yet we know that the love of God always protects, always trusts, always hopes, always perseveres, and never fails; and so, like Paul in Philippians, we "press on toward the goal to win the prize for which God has called [us] heavenward in Christ Jesus" (Phil. 3:14).

Paul tells us that love is to be our motivation for the exercise of spiritual gifts. This is "the most excellent way." In the ministry of healing, as we move in the power and authority of God we must always seek to protect those we minister to, encouraging them to trust in God with perseverance and hope that our prayers are heard and answered by our heavenly Father who loves us and has given us access to His throne of grace through His matchless Son, Jesus.

QUESTIONS AND REFLECTIONS

1. Have you ever seen someone trying to minister healing who is not motivated by the love of God? What was your inward reaction, and what were the results of their efforts?

2. Using First Corinthians 13:1–13, reflect on Paul's teaching that the more excellent way to minister is to operate in the gift of faith motivated by God's love. Think of an instance when you have done this, and reflect on the outcome.

PRAYER DIRECTIVE

Come quietly before the Lord and allow Him to help you identify those areas of deficiency in your life in the context of the love passage in First Corinthians 13. Then pray, asking God to come into your heart and replace your deficiencies with His sufficiency. Consider using the following prayer of confession:

> *Most merciful God, I confess that I have sinned against You in thought, word, and deed, by what I have done, and by what I have left undone. I have not loved You with my whole heart; I have not loved my neighbors as myself. I are truly sorry and I humbly repent. For the sake of Your Son Jesus Christ, have mercy on me and forgive me; that I may delight in Your will, and walk in Your ways, to the glory of Your name. Amen.[1]*

NOTE

1. *The Book of Common Prayer* (New York: The Church Hymnal Corporation, 1979), 79. Wording changed slightly to reflect individual prayer rather than corporate prayer.

REVELATORY GIFTS

Now to each one the manifestation of the Spirit is given for the common good.
To one there is given through the Spirit the message of wisdom, to another
the message of knowledge by means of the same Spirit, to another faith by
the same Spirit, to another gifts of healing by that one Spirit, to another
miraculous powers, to another prophecy, to another distinguishing between
spirits, to another speaking in different kinds of tongues, and to still another the
interpretation of tongues. All these are the work of one and the same Spirit, and
He gives them to each one, just as He determines (1 Corinthians 12:7–11).

Revelatory gifts have an integral part in the ministry of healing, and we do well to discover the ways of God regarding His revelatory gifts. Notice in the above passage that Paul tells us that each one of the manifestations of the Spirit is given for the common good. Take, for instance, words of knowledge. They are supernatural revelation from the Holy Spirit and, when spoken during times of ministry, can have a powerful impact on the recipient (for their good). In the gospels we find instances when God uses words of knowledge in particular situations. In Mark 2:8, "Immediately Jesus knew in His spirit that this was what they were thinking in their hearts." In John 1:47, Jesus speaks a word of knowledge to Nathaniel, who as a result immediately recognizes Jesus as the Messiah. In the gospel of Luke, the baby John leaps in his mother Elizabeth's womb when her cousin Mary (the mother of Jesus) greets her.

These revelatory gifts cannot be attained by human effort, and they are not constant. They cannot be created by spiritual exercises. They are gifts from God, given so that His will may come about in situational moments. They allow us to know the will of God in a specific situation, thereby causing great faith for answered prayer for a miracle or healing. Flowing out of our relationship with Jesus, gifts of His unmerited favor come often to those who expect them, understand how to recognize them, and who make a point to look for them.

QUESTIONS AND REFLECTIONS

The woman said to him, "Sir, give me this water so that I won't get thirsty and have to keep coming here to draw water." He told her, "Go, call your husband and come back." "I have no husband," she replied. Jesus said to her, "You are right when you say you have no husband. The fact is, you have had five husbands, and the man you now have is not your husband. What you have just said is quite true." "Sir," the woman said, "I can see that you are a prophet" (John 4:15–19).

With a word of knowledge, Jesus brought the life-giving message of the gospel to a Samaritan woman who then took it back to her village. As a result of this one word of knowledge, many in that village came to Christ. Has there been an instance when a word of knowledge you gave dramatically impacted someone's life? If so, what took place?

Read Acts 5:1–11 and reflect on the word of knowledge given to Peter regarding the activity of Ananias and Sapphira. God knew what was going on in their hearts, and through Peter He revealed Himself to this husband and wife who were attempting to profit from dishonor, using them as an example that the Spirit of the Lord cannot be deceived. Why is it important to continually seek revelation from God as you are ministering to someone?

REFLECTION

Follow the way of love and eagerly desire spiritual gifts, especially the gift of prophecy (1 Corinthians 14:1).

But everyone who prophesies speaks to men for their strengthening, encouragement and comfort (1 Corinthians 14:3).

Read First Corinthians 14:1 and 3, reflecting on Paul's exhortation to the Church to use the gifts for the edification of the body (the Church). Now, reflect on those gifts you personally see in operation in the Church today that are being used for the edification of the body of Christ, noting how they are specifically impacting people—strengthening, encouragement, comfort, etc.

What gifts would you personally like to see in operation in your church that are not there now? Why? Spend time now in small groups, praying for spiritual gifts in your life and your church community.

GOD INTENDS TO HEAL

God is intentional about healing, and He will act in
ways that express His intentionality.

One generation shall laud your works to another, and shall declare
your mighty acts…all your faithful shall bless you. They shall speak
of the glory of your kingdom, and tell of your power, to make known
to all people your mighty deeds (Psalm 145:4,10–12 NRSV).

We serve a mighty and glorious God who desires that we draw near to Him and learn His ways, and the surest path to learning God's ways begins by studying His mighty deeds as found in the Scriptures. It is here that we find the strong connection between an intimate knowledge of God's ways and His glory. The Psalms in particular almost shout of the glory of God. "We will not hide them from their children; we will tell the next generation the praiseworthy deeds of the Lord, His power, and the wonders He has done" (Ps. 78:4). "I will meditate on all your works and consider all your mighty deeds. Your ways, O God, are holy" (Ps. 77:12-13). "O give thanks to the Lord; call upon His name, make known His deeds among the peoples" (Ps. 105:1 ESV).

There is a strong correlation between the level of faith and the level of healing. During Jesus' earthly ministry, a high level of expectation that He would heal developed as a result of the miracles He performed. The woman with the issue of bleeding had faith to believe if she so much as touched the hem of His garment she would be healed, and she was. The Roman centurion believed that if Jesus simply said the word his servant would be healed from afar, and he was. We need to see this same level of faith and expectation for the miraculous in the Church today, and yet wrong teaching makes it difficult.

REFLECTIONS

The Lord would speak to Moses face to face, as a man speaks with his friend. Then Moses would return to the camp, but his young aide Joshua son of Nun did not leave the tent. Moses said to the Lord, "You have been telling me, 'Lead these people,' but you have not let me know whom you will send with me. You have said, 'I know you by name and you have found favor with me.' If you are pleased with me, teach me your ways so I may know you and continue to find favor with you. Remember that this nation is your people." The Lord replied, "My Presence will go with you, and I will give you rest." Then Moses said to him, "If your Presence does not go with us, do not send us up from here. How will anyone know that you are pleased with me and with your people unless you go with us? What else will distinguish me and your people from all the other people on the face of the earth?" And the Lord said to Moses, "I will do the very thing you have asked, because I am pleased with you and I know you by name." Then Moses said, "Now show me your glory" (Exodus 33:11–18).

Moses understood the importance of learning God's ways—directly from God—in order to find favor with Him. Reflecting on Exodus 33:11–18, there are several things to be learned from this dialogue between Moses and God. We need the real presence of God in order to relate to Him. We need to come into a place of intimacy with God. Notice that Moses wasn't willing to settle for intimacy with God—he wanted to see God's glory too, as part of a greater intimacy. It is difficult to co-labor with God if we don't have an intimate relationship with Him.

1. Take some time today to reflect on the intimacy of your relationship with God. If you earnestly desire a deeper relationship with Him, seek Him and you will find Him. Call on Him and He will draw near. Don't wait another day. Do it now!

The Israelites were too frightened to have an intimate relationship with God, so they made Moses their intermediary. Jesus has removed the "curtain" separating God from man. We can now approach God with confidence that He will hear our prayers and answer.

2. If there are needs in your life that you would like to bring to God, but you have been hesitant to approach Him, remember the words of Hebrews 4:15-16: *"For we do not have a high priest who cannot sympathize with our weaknesses, but One who has been tempted in all things as we are, yet without sin. Therefore let us draw near with confidence to the throne of grace, so that we may receive mercy and find grace to help in time of need"* (NASB). Take time now to approach your loving heavenly Father's throne of grace with confidence.

PRAYER

Dear Lord, give us courage to approach Your throne of grace boldly, in the name of Your Son, that me might receive Your mercy and empowerment to reap a rich harvest for Your Kingdom here on earth.

Ask and it will be given to you; seek and you will find; knock and the door will be opened to you (Matthew 7:7).

A HISTORY OF HEALING THEOLOGY AND SUPERNATURAL DEMONSTRATION

There is a difference between confirming the gospel and confirming doctrines and Scripture. A study of the New Testament indicates that the function or purpose of healings and miracles is to be part of the expression of the gospel. The gifts, including healings and miracles, are part of the "good news" of the in-break of the Kingdom of God and are to continue until Jesus' second coming. They display the mercy and love of God as found in Jesus and should never have been separated from His gospel.

For I would not dare say anything except what Christ has accomplished through me to make the Gentiles obedient by word and deed, by the power of miraculous signs and wonders, and by the power of God's Spirit. As a result, I have fully proclaimed the good news about the Messiah from Jerusalem all the way around to Illyricum (Romans 15:18-19 HCSB).

SESSION 4 SUMMARY

As we look back over the first 400 or more years of church history, we hear the early fathers collectively saying, "Miracles have not stopped. They still occur today!" So why then do we have such division within the Church today on this issue? How did the Church, which witnessed so much healing its first thousand years, become so closed and skeptical about this vital ministry? I believe we have erred by focusing the redemption we have in Christ almost totally in the future, while making only moral changes available in this present life. This was not the understanding or the focus of the early Church.

The early community of Christians believed in a present power not only for moral change, but also for authority over demons, power over sickness and disease, and the experience of the reality of spiritual gifts in their lives, especially in the corporate life of gathered congregations. Today, we have emptied the Atonement (the cross) of its full effect by an understanding that is correct as far as it goes—substitutionary atonement. Unfortunately, this understanding does not go far enough. It must be balanced by other understandings of the atoning work of Jesus on the cross, especially the *Christus Victor* understanding of atonement. It is only when we comprehend the fullness of what occurred on the cross that we can fully appreciate all that Jesus did for us in His scourging and crucifixion.

The Anti-Nicene fathers preached a Jesus who cared about releasing captives from demonic influences as well as freeing people from their bondage to sin. In short, they preached the good news. They preached a Jesus of compassion who cared about the sickness of a man's body as well as his soul. God is much more interested in whether or not we are relationally correct with Him than in whether or not we have all our doctrinal ducks in a row. Rather than looking at the consequences of sin's curse as the work of the enemy that the Church has the authority and power to come against—to continue the work of Christ who came "to destroy the devil's work" (1 John 3:8)—Christians began to see all things as foreordained and therefore to passively accept what they believed to be God's will. Ultimately, this shift from a warfare worldview to a blueprint worldview would have a distinctly negative impact upon the theology of healing in the Church.

DISCUSSION QUESTIONS

1.   For the last 500 years liberal and cessationist Protestant pastors have preached a powerless gospel, teaching North American and European churches not to believe or expect the gifts of healing and working of miracles in the Church because they no longer exist. How would you refute this liberal and cessationist teaching based on your personal experience?

2.   Matthew 4:23 says, "Jesus went throughout Galilee, teaching in their synagogues, preaching the good news of the kingdom, and healing every disease and sickness among the people." When we emphasize the soul without concern for our physical bodies, how does that run contrary to the gospel of Jesus?

3.   Read Matthew 8:17: "This was to fulfill what was spoken through the prophet Isaiah: 'He

took up our infirmities and carried our diseases.'" Elsewhere in his gospel, Matthew uses the healings of Jesus as proof of His (Jesus') messianic claims. Do you think God intends the gospels to be mere history, or is He speaking prophetic testimony through the history of His Church? Why is this important?

4.   Read Matthew 4:4 and Second Timothy 3:14–17 and then consider that the age of reason and intellectualism replaced divine revelation and experience with "right reasoning"—if it couldn't be explained by human reasoning, it didn't happen. How does right reasoning run contrary to the nature of Christianity as revelation?

5.   Referencing Matthew 12:29 and Mark 3:27, Randy makes the statement that the energies of God make the power and presence of God tangible today and are the means by which the "strong man's house is plundered." Who is the "strong man" and how do we plunder his house according to the temptation of Jesus (see Matthew 4; Mark 1:9–13)?

GROUP ACTIVATION EXERCISES

This is what the Lord says, He who made the earth, the Lord who formed it and established it—the Lord is His name: "Call to me and I will answer you and tell you great and unsearchable things you do not know" (Jeremiah 33:2-3).

Using Jeremiah 33:2-3 as your focus, break up into small groups of two or three and share your experiences of church doctrine regarding divine healing. Then pray and ask God to lead you into greater revelation of His great desire to heal through the finished work of His Son, Jesus.

PRAYER

O Father, open our minds to greater revelations of your heart of love as expressed in Your matchless Son, Jesus Christ, who stretched out His arms on the cross and gave Himself up for us, for our redemption and healing. May Your truths take root in our hearts so that we can fully embrace all that was accomplished on the cross and learn to walk in the power and authority given to us in Your precious Holy Spirit. Amen.

WEEKLY READING ASSIGNMENT

Read Chapters 9 and 10 in *Authority to Heal* and be sure and complete your study guide assignments.

SESSION NOTES

EARLY CHURCH FATHERS
AND DIVINE HEALING

Divine healing, a river which has flowed throughout the 2000-year history of the Church, was reduced to a small stream within Protestantism for about 500 years but never dried up completely. In the last hundred years it has become a raging river, stronger and more powerful than in any other century of the Church.

> *On the last and greatest day of the Feast, Jesus stood and said in a loud voice, "If anyone is thirsty, let him come to me and drink. Whoever believes in me, as the Scripture has said, streams of living water will flow from within him." By this He meant the Spirit, whom those who believed in him were later to receive* (John 7:37–39).

The river of God is a powerful metaphor in Scripture that depicts the spiritual life available to all believers. In the Old Testament God gave His prophets visions of this great outpouring of His spiritual river. Ezekiel saw a vision of God's divine river flowing out from the temple. "Fruit trees of all kinds will grow on both banks of the river. Their leaves will not wither, nor will their fruit fail. Every month they will bear, because the water from the sanctuary flows to them. Their fruit will serve for food and their leaves for healing" (Ezek. 47:12). Zechariah saw the same river: "On that day living water will flow out from Jerusalem, half to the eastern sea and half to the western sea, in summer and in winter" (Zech. 14:8). Jeremiah gave a stern warning to the people of God not to foolishly try to establish their own sources of spiritual power: "My people have committed two sins: They have forsaken me, the spring of living water, and have dug their own cisterns, broken cisterns that cannot hold water" (Jer. 2:13).

For hundreds of years the Church Jesus died to establish did forsake God's powerful flow of living water, turning instead to wrong doctrine with the result that many fled to the occult seeking the power they couldn't find in the Church. One of the versions the occult takes today can be found in the New Age movement in all its permutations. The vast majority of those in the occult today (witchcraft, Freemasonry, and New Age) come from a Christian background. That alone gives us a frightening picture of the powerless Church.

It is imperative that we allow God's divine river to flow full force in His Church once again. We cannot stand against the spirit of the age outside of God's power and authority. Many of the early church fathers gave strong witness to God's mighty river of divine healing, and yet so many in the Church are ignorant of this aspect of church history. We have a rich history of healing, and it needs to be taught in the Church today—in our seminaries, Bible schools, and from the pulpit.

REFLECTIONS AND QUESTIONS

The main impediment to the flow of God's healing in the Church comes from cessationist doctrine, which is the belief that all the healings and miracles in the Bible are historical. The difficulty for cessationists is that their doctrine is not substantiated by the facts of history. An examination of the history of the Church and the biblical and theological foundations of healing repudiates cessationism.

The "manifestation" and "power" gifts did not die out with the last of the original apostles, and Scripture bears witness to this truth. These "gifts" were given to the Church at Pentecost and have remained available to all believers throughout the history of the Church, and many have appropriated them to the glory of God.

1. Reflecting on your reading of Chapter 9 in *Authority to Heal*, how does the history of the early Church and the church fathers line up with what you have been taught about church history?

The Anti-Nicene fathers preached a Jesus who cared about releasing captives from demonic influences as well as freeing people from their bondage to sin. In short, they preached the good news. They preached a Jesus of compassion who cared about the sickness of a man's body as well as his soul. The gifts of God's manifest power are core elements of the gospel of salvation to the whole man, not "emotional esoteric experiences" as some would try and characterize the signs and wonders in the history of the Church down to the present day.

2. What is your personal experience of the Church's reaction to the manifestations of God's spiritual gifts? How has this impacted your ministry?

DOCTORS OF THE CHURCH

Historical testimony to the Spirit's ongoing gifts can be found in the writings of Theophilus of Antioch (died c. 181), Arnobius and Lactantius from near the end of the Ante-Nicene period (300–325), and Quadratus, one of the earliest apologists who wrote in Rome that the works of the Savior had continued to his time and that the continued presence of men who had been healed left no question as to the reality of physical healing.

> *And I will ask the Father, and He will give you another Counselor to be with you forever—the Spirit of truth. The world cannot accept him, because it neither sees him nor knows him. But you know him, for He lives with you and will be in you* (John 14:16-17).

Throughout history the power and authority of the Holy Spirit has been available to all believers. In this passage from the gospel of John, Jesus tells us that the Holy Spirit will be with us *forever.* And then, with a word of knowledge, Jesus tells us that the world (which includes the Church) will reject the Holy Spirit because they are blind to see Him and deaf to knowledge of Him. The truth of Jesus' words is evident in the history of the Church and the world. But the most important truth in this passage that we need to cleave to is that the Holy Spirit will be with us forever. Forever means forever—permanent, always, without end.

A full examination of church history reveals that many of our early church fathers and doctors of the Church gave testimony to charismatic experiences and expressions more than 100 years after Christ's death and resurrection, and the death of the last of the apostles. From A.D. 296–393, spiritual leaders of the Church such as Athanasisu wrote of healings that occurred during his lifetime. Gregory of Nazianzus, Basil the Great, and Gregory of Nyssa all documented supernatural physical healings in the history of the Church.

REFLECTIONS AND QUESTIONS

And if the Spirit of him who raised Jesus from the dead is living in you, He who raised Christ from the dead will also give life to your mortal bodies through His Spirit, who lives in you (Romans 8:11).

Read John 14:15–31, focusing on the promised Holy Spirit that lives within you. How does an unshakable knowledge of the promise and presence of the Holy Spirit impact the way you understand church history, particularly in the context of the ministry of healing?

THE FULLNESS OF THE SUPREMACY OF CHRIST

The early community of Christians believed in a present power not only for moral change but also for authority over demons, power over sickness and disease, and the experience of the reality of spiritual gifts in their lives, especially in the corporate life of gathered congregations. They understood the supremacy of Christ.

> *He is the image of the invisible God, the firstborn over all creation. For by him all things were created: things in heaven and on earth, visible and invisible, whether thrones or powers or rulers or authorities; all things were created by him and for him. He is before all things, and in him all things hold together. And He is the head of the body, the church; He is the beginning and the firstborn from among the dead, so that in everything He might have the supremacy. For God was pleased to have all His fullness dwell in him, and through him to reconcile to himself all things, whether things on earth or things in heaven, by making peace through His blood, shed on the cross* (Colossians 1:15–20).

As we reflect on Colossians 1:15–20, we see a full picture of the identity of Christ. Jesus is supreme in all creation, reflecting and revealing the glory of God. He is supreme over all principalities, powers, and authorities. Jesus is the totality of God, embodying all of His attributes *and powers*. What we so often fail to understand is that this same Jesus lives in us. The fruits of His sacrifice are available to us. Jesus has all authority in heaven and on earth, and He invites us to appropriate that authority as we participate with Him in His commissionings.

The early Church understood the fullness of the supremacy of Christ. At one time God's gifts flowed throughout the Church, giving testimony to His presence and power and glory. But the further away we got from the resurrection, the further away we went from the truth of the fullness of the supremacy of Christ. We still understand part of His supremacy, but we have relegated the rest to the dustbin of history.

It is time for the bride of Christ to stop limping around with a partial quiver. We must once again take hold of everything Jesus makes available to us and stop being a pitiful bride.

REFLECTIONS

Then I heard what sounded like a great multitude, like the roar of rushing waters and like loud peals of thunder, shouting: "Hallelujah! For our Lord God Almighty reigns. Let us rejoice and be glad and give him glory! For the wedding of the Lamb has come, and His bride has made herself ready. Fine linen, bright and clean, was given her to wear" (Revelation 19:6–8).

Jesus, the King of all creation, will return for a victorious bride. The Church today is in a season of preparation with an explosion of the miraculous in the ministry of healing and deliverance and salvation. The harvest is plentiful and the workers are few! You can be among those raised up and sent forth to labor alongside Jesus in the harvest field of the earth. If you are feeling His call on your heart, press in, asking Him to make you ready.

PRAYER

Father, my heart is willing and I am listening for you. Call my name and I will answer you, Lord! Turn over the dry ground within me, making me ready to receive the life-giving rain of Your Spirit, so that I may produce Your fruit in season to the glory of Your mighty name. Amen.

WHY THE REFORMERS REJECTED THE MIRACULOUS

The reformers cried out for a return to the objective authority of Scripture and, in the process, became quite anti-supernatural.

> *For the time will come when men will not put up with sound doctrine. Instead, to suit their own desires, they will gather around them a great number of teachers to say what their itching ears want to hear. They will turn their ears away from the truth and turn aside to myths* (2 Timothy 4:3-4).

The great Protestant reformers Calvin and Luther felt keenly compelled to challenge the authority of the Catholic Church, considering their (the Catholic Church's) claim to spiritual authority to be grossly illegitimate. Given the horrors of the day done in the name of God, it is not hard to understand their animosity. The unfortunate result of their challenge was a move away from the supernatural in the life of the Church. We are still dealing with the effects of this today.

The actions of the reformers and their impact on church doctrine, coupled with the Age of Reason and intellectualism that swept Europe in the sixteenth and seventeenth centuries, profoundly impacted the Church's interpretation of Scripture, radically changing the landscape of theology regarding the present-day supernatural works of God.

REFLECTIONS AND QUESTIONS

Blessed are those who hunger and thirst for righteousness, for they will be filled (Matthew 5:6).

Focusing on Second Timothy 4:3-4, reflect on how the initial integrity of the reformers morphed into a turning away from the truth of Scripture, and the warning this is to all believers.

What particular instances in your walk of faith have put you in danger of turning away from the truth of Scripture? In light of what you are now learning, how should you deal with these situations?

PRAYER

Create in me a pure heart, O God, and renew a steadfast spirit within me. Do not cast me from your presence or take your Holy Spirit from me (Psalm 51:10-11).

HEALING AS AN EXPRESSION OF THE GOSPEL

A study of the New Testament indicates that the function or purpose of healings and miracles is to be part of the expression of the gospel.

> *When Jesus landed and saw a large crowd, He had compassion on them and healed their sick* (Matthew 14:14).

There are dozens of miracles recorded in the four gospels and the book of Acts. Everywhere Jesus went, He performed miracles. The miraculous aspect of His ministry confounded and angered the Jewish leaders of His day and gave great hope to the people. The multidimensional aspect of the supernatural nature of God is reflected in everything about Jesus, especially the healing and miracles He performed.

People's minds and bodies were healed, bringing them into a place of sound doctrine and drawing them closer to God. Those who were outcasts found inclusion in the ministry of Jesus. His actions reflected the character of God and gave people a picture of the Kingdom of Heaven on earth. The great love and compassion of God was His strong motivation for healing. It is not possible to separate healing from the heart of God. How greatly it must grieve His heart that the Church lost its mandate to move in power and authority for the miraculous. One can only imagine that a full restoration of the supernatural in the life of the Church would bring great joy to the heart of God.

REFLECTIONS AND QUESTIONS

Very early in the morning, while it was still dark, Jesus got up, left the house and went off to a solitary place, where He prayed. Simon and his companions went to look for him, and when they found him, they exclaimed: "Everyone is looking for you!" Jesus replied, "Let us go somewhere else—to the nearby villages—so I can preach there also. That is why I have come." So He traveled throughout Galilee, preaching in their synagogues and driving out demons (Mark 1:35–39).

A full expression of the gospel always reveals the heart of God. Jesus tells us that He is an exact representation of the Father, and we know from Scripture that healing was central to His earthly ministry; therefore, healing is central to the heart of God. We have been commissioned to preach the gospel everywhere, to everyone. If we do not include God's supernatural healing as an expression of His gospel, we are not fully expressing the gospel. Without healing, we are only offering part of the gospel to those He sends us. Read Mark 1:35–39, reflecting in particular on verses 38 and 39. Jesus was the embodiment of the "good news" and He understood that truth. How can you become a fuller representation of the gospel using Jesus as your model?

HOW WE LOST OUR INHERITANCE

The evolution of Christian theology away from the New Testament emphasis on healing, exorcism, and miracles led to the practice of going so far as to deny their contemporary occurrence. The result of this is that now, when it comes to healing miracles, we have many unbelieving believers and believing unbelievers.

Believe me when I say that I am in the Father and the Father is in me; or at least believe on the evidence of the miracles themselves (John 14:11).

SESSION 5 SUMMARY

The powerful Church of Jesus Christ lost its authority to serve in power and its understanding of the gospel as the in-breaking of the Kingdom of God, abdicating the power and authority to push back the dominion of the god of this world through wrong theology regarding the supernatural activity of God in the world. This evolution of Christian theology away from the New Testament emphasis on healing and miracles went so far as to deny their contemporary occurrence. This unbelief springs from a combination of factors from within and outside the Church.

An examination of these factors in the history of the Church, in both Catholicism and Protestantism, is very revealing of the lack of validity of many of the arguments—they are simply not supported by Scripture. Healing has historically been one of the most controversial subjects of the Church, and its restoration in the life of the body of Christ is not without conflict. But God is faithful and not deterred by conflict. His glory shines brightly in the midst of battle. James

1:16–18 says, "Don't be deceived, my dear brothers. Every good and perfect gift is from above, coming down from the Father of the heavenly lights, who does not change like shifting shadows. He chose to give us birth through the word of truth, that we might be a kind of firstfruits of all He created." God is unchanging and ever faithful, and His supernatural empowerment for the working of miracles and healings in the Church today is evidence. He has unleashed His mighty river of healing on the earth today, making it harder and harder to deny the truth of His word.

DISCUSSION QUESTIONS

1. The combination of sociological factors highlighted in Chapter 11 contributed to the loss of the Church's supernatural power and authority to heal. What sociological factors do you see today that are impacting the restoration of gifts in the life of the Church?

2. Both Catholicism and Protestantism developed theology that led the Church away from the truth of the Scriptures regarding the operation of the supernatural, with the result that the miraculous works of God today are being labeled by some as myth, legend, and even delusion. Once again the Messiah is fulfilling Isaiah 61, and once again religious authorities are rejecting His testimony. What is your understanding of the Isaiah 61 mandate?

3. Infant baptism has led to a decline of the miraculous in the Church by creating a separation between the baptismal rite and the experience of the Holy Spirit. As a result, many never experience the fullness of the Holy Spirit. What is your baptismal experience, and did it include the experience of the Holy Spirit?

4. The moral corruption of the Middle Ages spilled over into the Church, leading to the Church taking the ministry of healing out of the hands of the laity and placing it in the domain of the clergy, where it has tried to remain. How have you seen this play out in your own church experience? Do you agree or disagree?

5. Cessationist B.B. Warfield wrote extensively on the cessation of the miraculous in the church; however, his foundational arguments were faulty. After reading Chapter 13, what do you think of Warfield's arguments in light of the scriptural truth that the purpose of miracles is to express the gospel, not to validate or express correct doctrine?

GROUP ACTIVATION EXERCISES

When Jesus saw Nathanael approaching, He said of him, "Here is a true Israelite, in whom there is nothing false." "How do you know me?" Nathanael asked. Jesus answered, "I saw you while you were still under the fig tree before Philip called you."

Then Nathanael declared, "Rabbi, you are the Son of God; you are the King of Israel." Jesus said, "You believe because I told you I saw you under the fig tree. You shall see greater things than that." He then added, "I tell you the truth, you shall see heaven open, and the angels of God ascending and descending on the Son of Man" (John 1:47–51).

Reflecting on John 1:47–51, break up into small groups of two or three and spend time sharing with one another how a word of knowledge profoundly impacted you or someone you know or ministered to. Then, come back together as one large group and have a handful of people share what they shared in their smaller group. With these testimonies as examples, how can cessationism remain a valid argument?

WEEKLY READING ASSIGNMENT

Read Chapters 11, 12, and 13 in *Authority to Heal*, and be sure to do your study guide assignments this week.

SESSION NOTES

THE CONTROVERSY OF HEALING

Healing was the most controversial subject of the Protestant Church during the last twenty-five years of the nineteenth century.

But when the Pharisees heard this, they said, "It is only by Beelzebub, the prince of demons, that this fellow drives out demons" (Matthew 12:24).

Healing has been a controversial subject in the Church since Jesus began His earthly ministry. The people Jesus ministered to eagerly received the gifts of healing that God had for them, but those in power could not abide what was happening. They were greatly threatened and very quickly conspired to put a stop to Jesus, making all sorts of false accusations against Him. Today we would say the charges were "trumped up," that Jesus was framed. And He was, as part of God's big plan for the redemption of all mankind.

Because healing is so central to the heart of God and so central to the message of the gospel, is it any wonder that Satan fights so hard to keep it out of the Church?

The Kingdom of God does not adhere to the political correctness of the kingdoms of this world. Jesus was a very politically incorrect individual and still is. Those of us called to the ministry of healing in the Church quickly find ourselves swimming against the tide both inside and outside the Church. Oftentimes we will find ourselves fighting for the life of the Spirit of God to be allowed into our lives and into our churches.

If you have found yourself swimming against the tide, how has God equipped you to deal with this resistance?

REFLECTIONS AND QUESTIONS

In the Matthew 12:24 passage, it may seem a bit extreme for the Pharisees to try and associate Jesus' power and authority with that of the devil, but this same accusation has been hurled at believers who move in the supernatural power and authority of God throughout the history of the Church. They have been expelled, excommunicated, burned at the stake, marginalized, and demonized. This is still going on in the twenty-first century, believe it or not. If you are walking in supernatural manifestations of God's power and authority, you most likely have already experienced some of this prejudice. In third-world countries the prejudice often takes on the most extreme forms mentioned above.

Read Matthew 12:22–37. When Jesus was accused of performing miracles in the power of the devil, how did He respond? If someone has tried to shut down the working of the Holy Spirit in your life, what did they do, and how did you respond?

PRAYER

O Father, your grace is sufficient for me, for your power is made perfect in my weakness (2 Corinthians 12:9 paraphrased).

BAPTIZED BY WATER AND THE SPIRIT

If one does not appropriate baptismal faith as they grow up, there is the danger of never experiencing the fullness of the Holy Spirit that is to accompany our infant baptism.

> *Peter replied, "Repent and be baptized, every one of you, in the name of Jesus Christ for the forgiveness of your sins. And you will receive the gift of the Holy Spirit"* (Acts 2:38).

Infant baptism came into the Church and in many denominations has replaced adult baptism. While there is nothing wrong with infant baptism in and of itself, it does not afford the infant an opportunity to experience the Holy Spirit in the same way they would as an adult. Often people who are baptized as infants grow up never experiencing the fullness of the Holy Spirit.

Baptism is an act of divine grace. Jesus received this divine grace when He was baptized, and He commanded His disciples and all believers to baptize others. Baptism is grounded in the gospel and made available by the finished work of Christ on the cross. In the act of baptism, we die to self or sin, rise to newness of life in Christ, and receive the precious Holy Spirit. We are baptized by water and the Spirit (see John 3:5; Acts 2:38). The water symbolically washes us clean as the Holy Spirit enables us to participate in the death and resurrection of Christ. Equipped by God, we are to go forth to live a life of faith nourished by the Spirit.

REFLECTIONS AND QUESTIONS

> *Jesus answered, "I tell you the truth, no one can enter the kingdom of God unless he is born of water and the Spirit. Flesh gives birth to flesh, but the Spirit gives birth to spirit* (John 3:5-6).

If you have not yet experienced adult water baptism, prayerfully consider it now. Seek good counsel. Attending a baptism preparation class beforehand is an excellent way to more fully appreciate what you are about to undertake. Be ready to receive all that God has for you.

> *I baptize you with water. But one more powerful than I will come, the thongs of whose sandals I am not worthy to untie. He will baptize you with the Holy Spirit and with fire* (Luke 3:16).

> *For we are all baptized by one Spirit into one body—whether Jews or Greeks, slave or free—and we were all given the one Spirit to drink* (1 Corinthians 12:13).

In baptism we are regenerated by the Holy Spirit and incorporated into the Church. In this passage in Corinthians, Paul reminds us that there is no distinction in Christ because we all drink from the same Spirit. The ground is level at the foot of the cross because Jesus leveled the field.

Have you ever been tempted to feel even slightly superior when you operate in the gifts of the Spirit? How should you guard your heart against such a temptation?

PRAYER

> *O Lord, today may I draw water with rejoicing from your springs of salvation. May I make known your deeds among the peoples so that they remember that your name is exalted* (Isaiah 12:3-4 paraphrased).

ALL CAN PARTICIPATE

It is of note here that the Middle Ages, which was a period of moral corruption without correction, saw a decrease in healing and an increase in apathy and a lack of purity. This brought about the perception on the part of both clergy and laity that laity were not holy or good enough to be used for healing.

> *As for you, the anointing you received from him remains in you, and you do not need anyone to teach you. But as His anointing teaches you about all things and as that anointing is real, not counterfeit—just as it has taught you, remain in him* (1 John 2:27).

Given the moral corruption and hypocrisy that had crept into the Church by the Middle Ages, it is understandable that leadership wanted to take authority away from the laity and put it in the hands of the clergy. Unfortunately, this sent the Church down a path that was not scriptural.

Under the Old Covenant, not everyone was anointed for the work of the Lord. Under the New Covenant, all can be anointed by the Spirit to do the work of the Kingdom, but it is an uphill battle. Oftentimes the Church will initially welcome a visitation of the Spirit only to limit its impact. Charismatic expressions may be welcomed, only to be relegated to the "back room," out of sight and hopefully out of the minds of most congregants or not welcomed at all.

It is not a ministry office or a title that authorizes us to heal the sick. We are authorized to heal the sick through the name of Jesus Christ and the power of the Holy Spirit dwelling within us. As ministers of the gospel, filled and empowered by the Spirit of God, we must always and everywhere walk in unblemished integrity. This should be normative in the lives of all believers, but it is especially important when our actions are subject to heightened scrutiny. If we long to be allowed to participate, we must show ourselves worthy of the gospel of Jesus Christ in thought, word, and deed.

REFLECTIONS AND QUESTIONS

Some, however, made fun of them and said, "They have had too much wine." Then Peter stood up with the Eleven, raised his voice and addressed the crowd: "Fellow Jews and all of you who live in Jerusalem, let me explain this to you; listen carefully to what I say. These men are not drunk, as you suppose. It's only nine in the morning! No, this is what was spoken by the prophet Joel: 'In the last days, God says, I will pour out my Spirit on all people'" (Acts 2:13–17).

Physical manifestations of the Holy Spirit can be off-putting to those who are watching. When the human body encounters the power of the Spirit of the Creator of the universe, it often responds in ways that are unusual to the natural eye. Add to that someone suddenly speaking in another language, and you have a recipe for confusion. People don't understand what they are seeing and tend to react by rejecting what is happening. Many a move of God has been shut down when manifestations begin.

Read and reflect on Acts 2 in its entirety. This is one of the most significant events in the early Church outside of the gospel narrative, and it remains one of the most significant events in the life of the believer today.

How have you stewarded the Holy Spirit in you? Are there any instances where you behaved in a manner that was unworthy of Jesus in the midst of a Holy Spirit encounter, allowing the flesh to take over? If so, now is the time to come before God and repent of your behavior, remembering that repentance is actually a turning away from that which was ungodly to that which aligns with the Spirit of the Lord. "Blessed are those who hunger and thirst for righteousness, for they will be filled" (Matt. 5:6).

Jesus died so that we might enjoy freedom from the bondage of sin and death. Even though we fail at times to live fully in the high calling of Christ, we must remember that we are being transformed into His image from glory to glory, free in Christ.

Now the Lord is the Spirit, and where the Spirit of the Lord is, there is freedom. And we, who with unveiled faces all reflect the Lord's glory, are being transformed into His likeness with ever-increasing glory, which comes from the Lord, who is the Spirit (2 Corinthians 3:17-18).

CESSATIONISM

Miracles, healings, and signs and wonders done by the disciples down to this day testify to the truth of the gospel by confirming the in-breaking of the Kingdom of God with the coming of Jesus.

> *As a result, people brought the sick into the streets and laid them on beds and mats so that at least Peter's shadow might fall on some of them as he passed by. Crowds gathered also from the towns around Jerusalem, bringing their sick and those tormented by evil spirits, and all of them were healed (Acts 5:15-16).*

Cessationist thinking has permeated the Church for far too long, but it is rapidly losing ground. The flood of healings and miracles occurring around the globe can no longer be denied. God is pouring out His Spirit like a mighty rushing river, and it will soon overtake wrong doctrine and false teaching. Many who do not yet know Jesus will come to Him as a result of a miracle or healing. You don't have to be a believer to understand that you have seen a leg grow out or a blind eye see or a cancerous tumor fall from someone's body or a lame man walk, but you will most likely become one after such an experience.

God will advance His Kingdom on this earth, and the gates of hell will not prevail against it. The charismatic portion of the Church worldwide is growing exponentially. If this growth continues at its current pace, it will overtake the powerless Church in size and scope and cessationism will pale in comparison to the mighty river of God.

REFLECTIONS AND QUESTIONS

For no one can lay any foundation other than the one already laid, which is Jesus Christ (1 Corinthians 3:11).

Read First Corinthians 3 in its entirety, reflecting especially on verses 12-13, "If any man builds on this foundation using gold, silver, costly stones, wood, hay or straw, his work will be shown for what it is, because the Day will bring it to light. It will be revealed with fire, and the fire will test the quality of each man's work." Paul is telling the church in Corinth that only that which is built on the foundation of the truth of Scripture will stand the test of divine judgment. Any other foundation will prove to be weak and not up to the task.

From your own personal experience, what weaknesses do you see in the foundations of cessationist doctrine as described in Chapter 13 of *Authority to Heal*?

PRAYER DIRECTIVE

Praying the Scriptures is a marvelous way to release the power and authority of the living Word. Take a moment now to pray these verses from Psalm 118:

I will give thanks, for you answered me; you have become my salvation. The stone the builders rejected has become the capstone; the Lord has done this, and it is marvelous in our eyes (Psalm 118:21–23).

WILD FIRE VERSUS REAL FIRE

The strategy of Satan is to mix wild fire with real fire in order to take leaders into extremes, causing the move of God to fall into disrepute.

> *Don't be deceived, my dear brothers. Every good and perfect gift is from above, coming down from the Father of the heavenly lights, who does not change like shifting shadows. He chose to give us birth through the word of truth, that we might be a kind of firstfruits of all He created* (James 1:16–18).

There are some in the Church who have issued volatile teachings that warn of the dangers of offending the Holy Spirit with the strange fire of counterfeit worship. They seem to think that by adding the element of "offending the Holy Spirit," they give great weight to their argument, when in fact the weight of their own offense is slowly dragging them to the bottom of the pond. In light of the millions who have come to the saving knowledge of Jesus Christ in the current worldwide renewal, there is little validity to their argument.

"Real fire" from God is often accompanied by what seems to be unusual behavior, but those seeking to jump into the river of God have learned the wisdom of not throwing the baby out with the bathwater. They will take a bit of wild fire in order to get the real fire. They learn to steward well what they have been given with gentleness of heart, wisdom, and discernment, minimizing the wild fire while relishing the real fire.

REFLECTIONS AND QUESTIONS

> *Behold, I stand at the door and knock. If anyone hears my voice and opens the door, I will come in to him and eat with him, and He with me* (Revelation 3:20 ESV).

God is always waiting for us to respond to Him. He is the One standing outside the door knocking, waiting for us to hear His voice and open the door of our heart and invite Him in. Sometimes when we open the door, God doesn't look like we thought He would. The real fire standing on our doorstep can look a bit like strange fire at first glance. "But thanks be to God, who always leads us in triumphal procession in Christ and through us spreads everywhere the fragrance of the knowledge of him" (2 Cor. 2:14). God in His great love will take us with all of our doubts and fears and misunderstandings and fashion and shape us into His people if we will only allow Him in.

PRAYER DIRECTIVE

If you have closed the door of your heart because you saw something of God that didn't fit your impression of what He should look like, now is a good time to go back and open the door and let the King of glory come in. Kneel before Him and invite Him into your heart regardless of how that looks to the rest of the world, asking for His wisdom and discernment to know the real from the counterfeit.

Lift up your heads, O you gates; be lifted up, you ancient doors, that the King of glory may come in. Who is this King of glory? The Lord strong and mighty, the Lord mighty in battle. Lift up your heads, O you gates; lift them up, you ancient doors, that the King of glory may come in (Psalm 24:7–9).

RECLAIMING OUR AUTHORITY TO HEAL

Can there be any question that the mightiest moves of the Spirit, which have resulted in the greatest numbers of people coming to God, have been those times of revival characterized by powerful outpourings of spiritual gifts and manifestations of God's very presence?

In the last days, God says, I will pour out my Spirit on all people. Your sons and daughters will prophesy, your young men will see visions, your old men will dream dreams. Even on my servants, both men and women, I will pour out my Spirit in those days, and they will prophesy (Acts 2:17-18).

SESSION 6 SUMMARY

When reading the Act 2:17-18 passage, a translation of the original Greek reveals that Peter's reference to the "last days" means the "days of the Messiah." The dispensation of the Old Covenant ended with the advent of Jesus. We are now living in the days of the New Covenant—the days of the Messiah. In the Old Testament, God dispensed His Spirit in small amounts. In the book of Acts, God's Spirit poured out on all people, Jew and Gentile, and it has not ceased. This mighty river of God has ebbed and flowed, not due to a lack of God's power but to the receptivity of those receiving or rejecting it. Today we see an abundance of the gifts of the Spirit pouring out on willing believers resulting in a great increase in the miraculous, especially in the ministry of healing.

Signs of restoration began in the mid-1800s and continue into the twenty-first century. Periods of revival have survived despite the prejudice that still exists in the Church today. Seminaries and Bible colleges that once taught only cessationist liberal doctrine are now beginning to embrace the supernatural move of God that is happening all over the earth today. Classic denominations are seeing their efforts to evangelize eclipsed by Pentecostals who embrace this outpouring of the Holy Spirit's power and the restoration of the power ministries of the Holy Spirit, especially the gifts of healing, working of miracles, and deliverance. Knowledge of the compassionate heart of God is being restored to the Church and to the world it touches. It is nothing short of astounding to discover how significant this move of God, with its recapturing the gifts of the Spirit, is to the growth of the Church.

DISCUSSION QUESTIONS

1. Were you surprised to learn that *The Shantung Revival* by Mary Crawford was reprinted in 1970 with almost all of the phenomena of the Holy Spirit edited out? How does this make you feel about the validity of church history that you have been taught over the years?

2. The Second Great Awakening was characterized by physical manifestations of the Spirit that many found unsettling. Rather than looking at the fruit that came from these powerful touches of God on His Church, some chose to label them false and even dangerous. Have you personally experienced physical manifestations as a result of a touch from God or know someone who has? If so, what was the fruit of these experiences?

3. Randy points out that it is not healthy to allow prejudice to blind us to the reality of the power and authority of God, both historically and in the Church today. Is there any prejudice that is getting in the way of your own experience of God?

4. Many of the great men and women in the history of the Church who were looking for a restoration of a fully empowered, apostolic Church as seen in the days of the First Pentecost, focused their ministry on the grace, compassion, and truth of God found in the Bible. How would you like to see knowledge of the compassion of God restored to the Church today?

5. The doctrine of "Christ is Victor" means that the cross did not just secure our ultimate salvation but that all of Satan's power was met head-on and defeated, breaking the dominion of the curse. This is the fullness of our salvation. Does the work of the cross stop at substitutionary atonement for you, or does the scope of the cross go beyond? Explain.

GROUP ACTIVATION EXERCISES

The whole creation is on tiptoe to see the wonderful sight of the sons of God coming into their own (Romans 8:19 PNT).

Break up into small groups of two or three and share examples of how and where you see the gifts of the Spirit being recaptured by believers, with a focus on the fruits that are coming forth. Come back together as a large group and have one person from each group share your examples. Once everyone has shared, focus on the bigger picture of how God is moving to advance His Kingdom today.

PRAYER

Father, we thank you that we no longer need to live in bondage because Jesus has freed us from sin, making us servants of righteousness who eagerly await His final coming in glory. In this time between His first and second coming, we thank you for giving us the precious gift of the Holy Spirit, to empower us for the work of the Kingdom. We thank You that the Spirit is there for the asking, in generous measure, and that we, Your beloved sons and daughters, are coming into the fullness of who You created us to be—your people, walking in Your love and authority.

WEEKLY READING ASSIGNMENT

Read Chapter 14 in *Authority to Heal* and be sure to complete your study guide assignments for the week.

SESSION NOTES

TIMES OF REVIVAL

The New Testament gives us God's blueprint for revival by outlining seven characteristics that happen when God is at work in the hearts of His people. When you see these things happening, revival is usually imminent.

No one can come to me unless the Father who sent me draws him (John 6:44).

God loves to stir the hearts of His people, to arouse and awaken us from our sleep so that we may partner with Him to advance His glorious Kingdom here on earth. In the book of Ezra, God stirred the hearts of the Israelites as He called them to return to Jerusalem (Ezra 1:1). Once their hearts were stirred, they were ready to rebuild God's house.

Times of revival are historically characterized by specific ways in which God stirs the hearts of people. This stirring begins with salvation, which is followed by an infilling of the Holy Spirit. Next comes sound teaching on the Kingdom of God as people are fed with the "meat" of the gospel. Saved and filled with power and authority and the truth of God's word, believers are then sent out to advance the Kingdom and fulfill the Great Commission. As we go forth and share the "good news," a holy fear takes hold in the hearts of those receiving the gospel, and they in turn experience salvation and all it brings. In times of revival, we will see all of these things continuing, as God grows His Church.

REFLECTION AND QUESTIONS

1. Read Ezra 1:1–5, reflecting on how God stirred the hearts of His people to leave Babylon and return to Jerusalem and rebuild the temple. How hungry are you for more of God? What are you willing to do, to give up, in order to get more

of Him? Allow the Holy Spirit to break up the fallow ground in your heart, to prepare the soil, so that you are ready to receive all He has for you. Remember, nothing of God will come out of our hearts unless God does the stirring.

2. Read Ezra 8:22-23 and 31-32, reflecting on how the Israelites prepared for the journey and how God responded. How is God calling you to prepare for an encounter with Him? How do you think He will respond?

DAY TWO

SIGNS OF RESTORATION

Evangelicals began seeing healing in the mid-1800s, and from 1875 until 1900 healing was the most controversial subject of many denominations. God was revealing Himself in supernatural power in the midst of the most conservative, mainline denominations. Many of today's cessation-teaching churches were birthed in renewal movements marked by charismatic manifestations.

> *When evening came, many who were demon-possessed were brought to him, and He drove out the spirits with a word and healed all the sick. This was to fulfill what was spoken through the prophet Isaiah: "He took up our infirmities and carried our diseases"* (Matthew 8:16-17).

The gospels are full of the healing miracles of Jesus. The mandate to heal and the evidence of God's power and authority in the life of believers have never left the Church despite the efforts of many. When God's mighty presence comes, we often see it accompanied by charismatic manifestations. These are signs of His restoration. But just as those in Jesus' time could not recognize Him, so it is today. Unwillingness to receive God when He comes has resulted in many lost opportunities, but God will not be stopped. Signs of restoration are plentiful in the history of the Church down to the present day. We just need to know where to look for them.

REFLECTION

Read Acts 2 in its entirety, giving particular attention to verses 13–41. In these passages we find the apostle Peter, not typically an eloquent speaker, addressing a crowd of naysayers immediately after God has poured out His promised Holy Spirit on the fledgling Church. With a boldness that comes from the empowerment of the Spirit, Peter addressed what appeared to be fleshly manifestations and presented the gospel, followed by an exhortation to repentance and baptism.

Some, however, made fun of them and said, "They have had too much wine."

Then Peter stood up with the Eleven, raised his voice and addressed the crowd: "Fellow Jews and all of you who live in Jerusalem, let me explain this to you; listen carefully to what I say. These men are not drunk, as you suppose. It's only nine in the morning! No, this is what was spoken by the prophet Joel:

"'In the last days, God says, I will pour out my Spirit on all people. Your sons and daughters will prophesy, your young men will see visions, your old men will dream dreams. Even on my servants, both men and women, I will pour out my Spirit in those days, and they will prophesy. I will show wonders in the heaven above and signs on the earth below, blood and fire and billows of smoke. The sun will be turned to darkness and the moon to blood before the coming of the great and glorious day of the Lord. And everyone who calls on the name of the Lord will be saved.'

"Men of Israel, listen to this: Jesus of Nazareth was a man accredited by God to you by miracles, wonders and signs, which God did among you through him, as you yourselves know. This man was handed over to you by God's set purpose and foreknowledge; and you, with the help of wicked men, put him to death by nailing him to the cross. But God raised him from the dead, freeing him from the agony of death, because it was impossible for death to keep its hold on him. David said about him:

"'I saw the Lord always before me. Because He is at my right hand, I will not be shaken. Therefore my heart is glad and my tongue rejoices; my body also will live in hope, because you will not abandon me to the grave, nor will you let your Holy One see decay. You have made known to me the paths of life; you will fill me with joy in your presence.'

"Brothers, I can tell you confidently that the patriarch David died and was buried, and his tomb is here to this day. But he was a prophet and knew that God had promised him on oath that He would place one of his descendants on his throne. Seeing what was ahead, he spoke of the resurrection of the Christ, that He was not abandoned to the grave, nor did His body see decay. God has raised this Jesus to life, and we are all witnesses of the fact. Exalted to the right hand of God, He has received from the Father the promised Holy Spirit and has poured out what you now see and hear. For David did not ascend to heaven, and yet he said,

"'The Lord said to my Lord: "Sit at my right hand until I make your enemies a footstool for your feet."'

"Therefore let all Israel be assured of this: God has made this Jesus, whom you cruci-
fied, both Lord and Christ."

When the people heard this, they were cut to the heart and said to Peter and the other
apostles, "Brothers, what shall we do?"

Peter replied, "Repent and be baptized, every one of you, in the name of Jesus Christ
for the forgiveness of your sins. And you will receive the gift of the Holy Spirit. The
promise is for you and your children and for all who are far off—for all whom the
Lord our God will call." With many other words he warned them; and he pleaded with
them, "Save yourselves from this corrupt generation." Those who accepted his message
were baptized, and about three thousand were added to their number that day.

QUESTIONS

Verse 41 says, "Those who accepted his message were baptized, and about three thousand were added to their number that day." This verse encapsulates the essence of revival, which is that the Church grows as God works through ordinary people like Peter who are empowered by His Spirit.

1. Have you ever found yourself in a situation like Peter, when suddenly you received an empowerment of God's Spirit that enabled you to bring the gospel with power? (For most of us, this means witnessing to one person rather than a crowd.) Explain.

2. If you have not yet had this experience, prayerfully consider asking God for this kind of boldness. What would it look like in your life, and what roadblocks has the enemy thrown up to keep you from advancing the Kingdom in this way?

3. Why is it easy to bring the good news of the gospel until we get to the part about repentance?

THE FULLNESS OF OUR SALVATION

Sozo, the Greek word for "save," is used in the Bible to refer to not only the saving of the soul but, more often, for deliverance from demonization and physical and emotional healing. It was this understanding of the fullness of our salvation, embraced by the Pentecostals, that gave such spiritual power to their message.

> *If you confess with your mouth, "Jesus is Lord," and believe in your heart that God raised Him from the dead, you will be saved* (Romans 10:9 HCSB).

The Greek word *sozo* is a verb and means "to save, heal, deliver, preserve and protect, and be made whole." It is used more than 100 times in the New Testament, but unless you study the Greek meaning of words in the Bible you could miss the fuller meaning of *sozo*.

The definition of *sozo* encompasses the fullness of our salvation. Thanks be to God that He has given us so much through Jesus. We don't just get term life insurance with Jesus, we get whole life insurance—we don't have to wait until we die to benefit from the atonement. We can enjoy the living benefits made available to us now—salvation, healing, deliverance, and protection. It is God's intention that we be made whole and live in the fullness of everything He gives us *now*.

REFLECTION AND QUESTIONS

Let's take several Bible verses and insert the word *sozo*, remembering its full definition.

For since in the wisdom of God the world through its wisdom did not know him, God was pleased through the foolishness of what was preached to save [sozo] those who believe (1 Corinthians 1:21).

Then those who had seen what happened told the others how the demon-possessed man had been healed [sozo] (Luke 8:36 NLT).

And the prayer of faith will save [sozo] the one who is sick, and the Lord will raise him up. And if he has committed sins, he will be forgiven (James 5:15 ESV).

Jesus turned and saw her. "Take heart, daughter," He said, "your faith has healed you." And the woman was healed [sozo] from that moment (Matthew 9:22).

Clearly Jesus gives us so much. While our salvation is of utmost importance, we should never neglect everything else given to us by the finished word of the cross. To do so is to minimize what Jesus accomplished. He died so that we might have abundant life.

1. Are you living and ministering to others from that place of abundance found in Jesus? If not, what is standing in your way?

2. If so, how is this abundance manifesting in your life and those around you?

PRAYER

Father, when I am weak, make me strong. When I am timid, make me bold for You. Help me to understand that I am worthy by Your unlimited gift of grace to tell of Your love. May I joyfully receive the rich inheritance You have given me in Jesus. Amen.

DAY FOUR

THE COMPASSION OF GOD

Pentecostalism was preceded by forerunner leaders such as Charles Spurgeon (1834–1892), who were looking for the restoration of a fully-empowered, apostolic Church as seen in the days of the first Pentecost. The focus of Spurgeon's ministry was the grace, compassion, and truth of God found in the Bible. His ministry of healing was based totally on his understanding of the compassion of God toward His children.

> *And He passed in front of Moses, proclaiming, "The Lord, the Lord, the compassionate and gracious God, slow to anger, abounding in love and faithfulness, maintaining love to thousands, and forgiving wickedness, rebellion and sin" (Exodus 34:6-7).*

To have compassion is to be concerned for the suffering of others. God is the "Father of mercies and God of all comfort" (2 Cor. 1:3 ESV), and He is concerned with suffering. The Old Testament is resplendent with the compassion of God, yet we find the greatest display of His compassion in His Son, Jesus, in the New Covenant. In the gospels, Jesus is moved again and again by great compassion as He heals and delivers all who come to Him. His compassion is a direct reflection of the heart of His Father.

As God's Spirit moves upon the earth, His compassion is a hallmark of His presence. When we minister to the lost and broken in the power and authority of God, His compassion must always be at the forefront.

REFLECTION AND QUESTIONS

Read Matthew 14:14, Matthew 18:10–14, Matthew 20:29–34, and Luke 19:41-42, reflecting on the compassion of Jesus as He moved among the people.

When Jesus landed and saw a large crowd, He had compassion on them and healed their sick (Matthew 14:14).

See that you do not look down on one of these little ones. For I tell you that their angels in heaven always see the face of my Father in heaven. What do you think? If a man owns a hundred sheep, and one of them wanders away, will he not leave the ninety-nine on the hills and go to look for the one that wandered off? And if he finds it, I tell you the truth, he is happier about that one sheep than about the ninety-nine that did not wander off. In the same way your Father in heaven is not willing that any of these little ones should be lost (Matthew 18:10–14).

As Jesus and His disciples were leaving Jericho, a large crowd followed him. Two blind men were sitting by the roadside, and when they heard that Jesus was going by, they shouted, "Lord, Son of David, have mercy on us!" The crowd rebuked them and told them to be quiet, but they shouted all the louder, "Lord, Son of David, have mercy on us!" Jesus stopped and called them. "What do you want me to do for you?" he asked. "Lord," they answered, "we want our sight." Jesus had compassion on them and touched their eyes. Immediately they received their sight and followed him (Matthew 20:29–34).

As He approached Jerusalem and saw the city, He wept over it and said, "If you, even you, had only known on this day what would bring you peace—but now it is hidden from your eyes" (Luke 19:41-42).

1. How does God's heart of compassion as demonstrated in Jesus impact the way in which you minister to the lost and broken in your life?

2. If we are void of the compassion of God, can His Spirit move through us to touch others? Explain.

3. What is happening in Luke 19:41-42? Why is Jesus weeping?

4. In Matthew 18:11–14, Jesus explains how important each one of us is to God. How does that truth impact your heart?

PRAYER DIRECTIVE

Reflecting on God's heart of compassion, especially as it applies to you personally as found in Matthew 18:11–14, come before God and receive His Father's heart for you, asking Him for a full revelation of His great love for you.

THE RIVER OF GOD CONTINUES TO FLOW

It is nothing short of astounding to discover how significant this move of God, with its recapturing the gifts of the Spirit, has been to the growth of the Church since 1901.

> *The earth will be filled with the knowledge of the glory of the Lord, as the waters cover the sea* (Habakkuk 2:14).

There is no question that the mightiest moves of the Spirit have resulted in the greatest numbers of people coming to God during times of revival, characterized by powerful outpourings of spiritual gifts and manifestations of God's presence. The healing river of God's Spirit continues to flow throughout the earth today despite those who are more concerned with phenomena than with evangelism.

God's great river of revival is made up of many streams. As you read through Chapter 15 in *Authority to Heal*, you will find yourself on a quick "tour" of this river of God. Baptists, Pentecostals, Charismatics, and others all experience God's presence and power. Men and women like Charles Spurgeon, Maria Woodworth-Etter, John G. Lake, Smith Wigglesworth, Aimee Semple-McPherson, T.L. Osborne, Reinhard Bonnke, Heidi Baker, and Randy Clark received a powerful impartation from God before being powerfully used by God. God is eager to use you, and the way in which He chooses to do so will be unique. Your calling, whether it is big or small, is of great value and importance to God.

REFLECTION AND QUESTIONS

Take time to read Chapter 15 in *Authority to Heal*, paying particular attention to the historic revivals and the men and women who were part of them.

1. How does a fuller knowledge of God's Spirit manifesting in the earth throughout history impact you?

2. What person or ministry has brought a fresh touch of God into your life? What is the fruit of this touch?

If you are frustrated that your calling is not as "big" as that of people like Randy Clark or Heidi Baker, read the story of Saul's conversion in Acts 9:1–18, paying particular attention to verses 10–19. Notice that the calling of Ananias initially seemed small and insignificant, but the ramifications on his obedience resounded down through the ages in the history of the Church and the world. Ananias was used by God to bring Saul into a relationship with Jesus, and as we know Saul became Paul and was used mightily by God to build the Church.

In Damascus there was a disciple named Ananias. The Lord called to him in a vision, "Ananias!" "Yes, Lord," he answered. The Lord told him, "Go to the house of Judas on Straight Street and ask for a man from Tarsus named Saul, for he is praying. In a vision he has seen a man named Ananias come and place his hands on him to restore his sight." "Lord," Ananias answered, "I have heard many reports about this man and all the harm he has done to your saints in Jerusalem. And he has come here with authority from the chief priests to arrest all who call on your name." But the Lord said to Ananias, "Go! This man is my chose instrument to carry my name before the Gentiles and their kings and before the people of Israel. I will show him how much he must suffer for My name." Then Ananias went to the house and entered it. Placing his hands on Saul, he said, "Brother Saul, the Lord—Jesus, who appeared to you on the road as you were coming here—has sent me so that you may see again and be filled with the Holy Spirit." Immediately, something like scales fell from Saul's eyes, and he could see again. He got up and was baptized, and after taking some food, he regained his strength (Acts 9:10–19).

3. Have you ever received a directive from God that challenged or frightened you to such an extent that you refused God?

4. If such a refusal has caused your walk with the Lord to grow a bit cold, are you willing to allow Him to make you bold in the power of His Spirit?

PRAYER DIRECTIVE

Come Holy Spirit, and fill my heart and kindle in it the fire of Your love. Send forth Your Spirit through me in order that Your work of renewing the face of the earth can continue unabated until the glorious return of Jesus Christ! Amen.

A NEW PENTECOST

I believe God is going to breathe upon His whole Church, across all denominational lines, awakening all of us to His power and authority and bringing unity to the body—an ecumenism of the Spirit rather than doctrinal ecumenism. I believe that the recovery of the gifts of the Spirit and the authority this gives to all believers are so important to the heart of God for His Church that He is going to cause both Protestants and Catholics to pray for a new Pentecost, one in which the Church will awaken afresh to the importance of the recovery of the gifts. Because, without His presence and His power and His authority—apart from signs and wonders and the gifts of the Holy Spirit—many more of those who don't know Him will not be awakened to His truth. When so much has been made available to the Church, why should we settle for less? Jesus' authority to heal can be restored in this generation and for all the generations to come.

"Awake, O sleeper, and arise from the dead, and Christ will shine on you."
Look carefully then how you walk, not as unwise but as wise, making the
best use of the time, because the days are evil. Therefore do not be foolish,
but understand what the will of the Lord is (Ephesians 5:14–17 ESV).

SESSION 7 SUMMARY

Many today see a westernized Church that has fallen asleep to the fullness of the gospel of Jesus Christ, with methods of evangelism limited to debate and argument rather than augmented by God's gracelets of healing and working of miracles. The Church of God and of our Lord Jesus Christ, in all its many streams, needs a restoration of all of the early gifts. But this restoration will not come without effort. We must be willing to wrestle against years of tradition and theology that have changed the makeup of the Church; wrestle against the traditions of those who have confused the Church's understanding of itself. We must wrestle to awaken the sleeping Church in the West if we are to experience the fullness of the gospel in all the world.

We must press in for a new Pentecost, understanding that the devil fears our God-given power and authority to bring heaven to earth. He has worked hard to distract us from this by keeping us focused on heaven and forgiveness, hoping we will not notice the present reality of our authority.

DISCUSSION QUESTIONS

Others, like seed sown on good soil, hear the word, accept it, and produce a crop— thirty, sixty or even a hundred times what was sown (Mark 4:20).

Reflect on Mark 4:20, taking note of the type of ground seed needs to fall on in order to yield a rich harvest. In this parable, all the seeds are the same; it is the type of ground that they fall upon that determines the harvest, and so it is with us. God will sow His seeds in our hearts, and some will graciously receive them and allow them to grow into a plentiful harvest while others will not so graciously receive them, and as a result the harvest will be less or not at all.

1.   What type of ground have the seeds of God found in your heart?

2.   In Ephesians 5:14, Paul says, "Awake, O sleeper, and arise from the dead and Christ will shine on you." What is Paul saying in this verse? Why are we asleep, dead?

3.   In the first paragraph in the Conclusion of *Authority To Heal*, Randy points out that our methods of evangelism are so often limited to debate and argument rather than being augmented by God's gracelets of healing and working of miracles. How do you feel about this statement that apologetics alone does not advance the Kingdom of God?

4.   Randy points out that Satan and his demonic philosophies have been used to try and stop the fulfillment of Jesus' prayer, "Thy kingdom come, thy will be done, on earth as it is in heaven." Do you see it this way also or do you disagree, and if so, why?

GROUP ACTIVATION

The first Pentecost resulted in the phenomenal growth of the early Church. Break up into groups of three or four and take time to reflect on what a second Pentecost would look like today, in the twenty-first century, allowing a reasonable amount of time for discussion. Then come back together and have someone from each group share what your group came up with. Once everyone has shared, come before the Lord as a group and pray, asking God for a new Pentecost in your heart and for the Church.

PRAYER

O Father, we cry out for You to rise up now, stretching forth Your Spirit over us in demonstrations of power and authority, so that we may partner with You to bring Your Kingdom to bear on the kingdom of this world until all have heard the good news.

WEEKLY READING ASSIGNMENT

Read the Conclusion in *Authority to Heal* and be sure to complete your weekly study guide assignments.

SESSION NOTES

RESTORATION OF ALL OF THE EARLY GIFTS

The Church of God—the Church of our Lord Jesus Christ—with all of its many streams needs a restoration of all of the early gifts. This is the understanding of the Kingdom of God that we must wrestle for.

> *Now about spiritual gifts, brothers, I do not want you to be ignorant. …There are different kinds of gifts, but the same Spirit. There are different kinds of service, but the same Lord. There are different kinds of working, but the same God works all of them in all men* (1 Corinthians 12:1, 4–6).

REFLECTION

In this passage in First Corinthians, the apostle Paul demonstrates the diverse unity of spiritual gifts that come to us through the indwelling of the Holy Spirit. The word *working* translates from the Greek as "operational power." Read First Corinthians 12 in its entirety. Notice how verses 27–31 address the value of each gift in the context of the church. Paul is saying that the gifts are equally valid but have different value in the body of Christ. We are all called to serve according to the gift(s) we are given, each one serving in proportion to our gifts. The sum total of our gifts operating together enables the Church to reach its full potential in the world. Identify your spiritual gifts from the list below and how you are currently operating as part of the body. Remember, all are gifts of God's grace, ruled by His love.

- Wisdom

- Knowledge

- Faith

- Healing

- Miracles

- Prophecy

- Discerning spirits

- Tongues

- Interpretation of tongues

- Administration

- Helping

APOLOGETICS VERSUS AUTHORITY

My message and my preaching were not with wise and persuasive words,
but with a demonstration of the Spirit's power, so that your faith might
not rest on men's wisdom, but on God's power (1 Corinthians 2:4-5).

The apostle Paul was a well-educated man and an eloquent speaker, yet he understood that his words alone were not sufficient to turn the hearts of men to the truth of the gospel. The Kingdom of God advances in the power and authority of the Holy Spirit, not through human wisdom and effort. Yes, we are to partner with God, and we must put forth effort to do so, but our efforts must be accompanied by the power of the Holy Spirit if they are to accomplish God's purposes.

Just as He did for the early apostles, God will move miraculously today to demonstrate His gospel. The ministry of Heidi and Rolland Baker in Mozambique is one example. On a regular basis they experience physical healings, deliverances, people raised from the dead, and the multiplication of food. And God doesn't just use Heidi and Rolland. He works through the orphan children they take in, through short-term missionaries just like you—through all believers. The result of God's miraculous presence in Mozambique is causing a great shift in the spiritual. This once-Muslim nation now has many provinces that have been declared Christian.

REFLECTIONS AND QUESTIONS

1. When you think about your own spiritual walk, what has had the greatest impact on you—teaching and preaching or the power and presence of God manifesting in your life? Why?

2. As you look around at the ministries going on all over the world, which ones are most impactful for the Kingdom, and why are they making such an impact?

God did extraordinary miracles through Paul, so that even handkerchiefs and aprons that had touched him were taken to the sick, and their illnesses were cured and the evil spirits left them (Acts 19:11-12).

Paul met stiff resistance as he went about the work of establishing the Church. God knew that Paul would need supernatural demonstrations of power to do the work of the Kingdom. The same is true today—God knows you need His supernatural power and authority to advance His Kingdom, and He will willingly give it to you.

3. Are you willing to receive all that God has for you? What roadblocks are there in your life right now that prevent you from receiving the fullness of God?

4. How hungry are you for more of God in your life and ministry? What price are you willing to pay for more of God?

PRAYER DIRECTIVE

Come before the Father now and give your life afresh to Him with a heart willing to pay any price for His presence and power. Ask Him to stir up a godly hunger in you that cannot be satisfied by anything less than the fullness of Him. Refuse to settle for a testimony of His power and authority when you can taste it in your own life.

DOCTRINAL STRONGHOLDS

The weapons we fight with are not the weapons of the world. On the contrary, they have divine power to demolish strongholds. We demolish arguments and every pretension that sets itself up against the knowledge of God, and we take captive every thought to make it obedient to Christ (2 Corinthians 10:4-5).

In this passage, Paul is addressing the church in Corinth, where many false teachings had sprung up and were confusing and shaking the faith of the early believers. Paul's goal was to equip those believers with knowledge of the kind of battle they were fighting—a spiritual battle that cannot be won with the weapons of men. This kind of battle can only be won with divine power of the Holy Spirit that demolishes doctrinal strongholds that are coming against the knowledge of God.

It is interesting to note that Satan wasted no time trying to shut down the power gifts in the Church, using doctrinal strongholds aimed at stunting its (the Church's) growth. Satan has been about this destructive work since the Church was established, and He is still at work today, spreading his demonic philosophies in an attempt to rob the Church of its power and authority.

REFLECTIONS AND QUESTIONS

1. As you reflect on Second Corinthians 10:4-5, what doctrinal strongholds come to mind?

2. How difficult is it for you to "take captive every thought to make it obedient to Christ," and why is it so difficult?

3. If you could "tear down" just one doctrinal stronghold, what would it be?

PRAYER DIRECTIVE

Spend time with your loving heavenly Father now, asking Him to reveal any doctrinal strongholds in your life that need to be torn down. Pray and ask the Holy Spirit to come and empower you to take your every thought captive and make it obedient to Christ.

A GOSPEL OF FORGIVENESS AND POWER AND AUTHORITY

He told them, "This is what is written: The Christ will suffer and rise from the dead on the third day, and repentance and forgiveness of sins will be preached in His name to all nations, beginning at Jerusalem. You are witnesses of these things. I am going to send you what my Father has promised; but stay in the city until you have been clothed with power from on high" (Luke 24:46–49).

In these three verses we find the framework for the gospel—repentance and forgiveness of sins to all—and the promised Holy Spirit, who will empower us to take the message of the gospel forth into the world. There is no separation here, no delineation of any aspect of the gospel making one thing more important than another. Jesus does not say that forgiveness is where we are to put our focus, nor does He say that the power of the Holy Spirit is to be central. He brings it all together—forgiveness, power, and authority—telling us that we are to go forth with the whole package.

You will notice that the Holy Spirit has to open their minds to these truths. As their minds are opened to the reality of what Jesus accomplished, they understand the necessity of repentance, which brings forgiveness of sins. Jesus has made so much available to us, His bride, and yet we are willing to settle for less.

REFLECTIONS AND QUESTIONS

So often we struggle as believers, thrashing about, trying to figure out how to bring the good news, how to reach our neighbor, our sister or brother, how to advance God's Kingdom in the midst of a hurting and broken world that seems to be spinning out of control more every day. We wring our hands and feel despair and seem to forget who we are. We forget about the One who lives in us. We forget about the promised Holy Spirit—the One the Father did indeed send to us, who is still here with us, ready to empower us for every challenge.

1. Why do you think we are so willing to settle for less?

2. What would it look like in your life to go after the fullness of the gospel?

3. Do you think it grieves the heart of Christ that He gives us so much and we settle for less? What do you think is His remedy for such grief?

ON EARTH AS IT IS IN HEAVEN

Our Father in heaven, hallowed be your name, your kingdom come,
your will be done on earth as it is in heaven (Matthew 6:9-10).

As Jesus teaches us to pray to God the Father, He tells us to call that which is in heaven to become present on the earth. We are to call for the Kingdom of God to manifest on the earth just as it is in heaven, and we can do this because Jesus has made it possible. Before the advent of Christ, prayers were lifted up for the promised Messiah to come. The good news is that He has come! Jesus has come in the flesh. The Kingdom of God has come to earth in Jesus Christ, and upon His glorious return to heaven we have been sent the precious Holy Spirit to empower us to call for that which is available to us to become present—for the Kingdom of God to manifest on the earth as it is in heaven. This is such glorious good news that the body of Christ should be shouting it from the rooftops!

We have been given so much and yet we settle for so little, but it is not too late—Jesus' authority to heal is still available to us and can be restored in this generation and for all the generations to come. It is there for the asking for all believers. All we need do is reach out and take hold of everything that Jesus has to offer.

REFLECTION

Paul's prayer for the church in Ephesus is so applicable to believers in today's Church. As you reflect on the words of Paul, press in for all that God has for you so that you too may walk in the fullness of Christ in you, the hope of glory.

For this reason I kneel before the Father, from whom His whole family in heaven and on earth derives its name. I pray that out of His glorious riches He may strengthen you with power through His Spirit in your inner being, so that Christ may dwell in your hearts through faith. And I pray that you, being rooted and established in love, may have power, together with all the saints, to grasp how wide and long and high and deep is the love of Christ, and to know this love that surpasses knowledge—that you may be filled to the measure of all the fullness of God.

Now to him who is able to do immeasurably more than all we ask or imagine, according to His power that is at work within us, to him be glory in the church and in Christ Jesus throughout all generations, for ever and ever! Amen (Ephesians 3:14–21).

GOD WANTS TO USE YOU

God is looking for people through whom He can show Himself strong. He needs committed believers who are totally surrendered and yielded to His will—ones who are so hungry for God that they are willing to "go anywhere and do anything" if God will just use them.

For the eyes of the Lord range throughout the earth to strengthen those whose hearts are fully committed to him (2 Chronicles 16:9).

SESSION 8 SUMMARY

In a number of Randy's books (see *Lighting Fires* and *Open Heaven: Are You Thirsty?*) he has shared how he experienced failure and rejection, and yet he was so hungry for a deeper relationship with God and to be used by God that he persisted even in the face of great opposition. Although some said Randy would never be used by God, Scripture does not agree with them. God will use anyone He chooses, regardless of the opinions of man, because God knows the heart. He knows who really hungers and thirsts for righteousness for His name's sake.

If you recall from the story of the Samaritan woman at the well, she was not a well-respected person in her community, and yet that didn't seem to matter to God. He saw the brokenness and hunger in her heart and used her to bring her entire village and the surrounding region to Jesus. God is not looking for perfect vessels. If we let Him, He will take our "old wineskins" and make us new so that we can carry the good news.

DISCUSSION QUESTIONS

Reflect on John 4:4–26, the story of Jesus' encounter with the Samaritan woman at the well. Notice that Scripture says that it was about the sixth hour when Jesus sat down by the well. It was an odd time of day for a woman to come alone to the well. Normally women of that day and time and place would come early in the morning to draw the water they would need for their daily tasks, and they would typically come together. But this woman had come alone, later in the day. Perhaps, because she was an outcast in her village, she avoided those times of day when the other women would be there.

This session is designed to take you through a study of Scriptures that provide ample evidence that God will use anyone He chooses, even you or me, even when we have fallen or failed, or just have no particularly impressive credentials in the eyes of the world.

1. Have you ever felt like an outcast in some way, like God would never use you for ministry? How do you think God sees you?

2. What does God see in your heart in terms of passion for Him and desperation to be used by Him?

3. In Second Chronicles 16:9, the Greek translation for the word *range* means to look intently. How would it feel to you if you realized God was looking intently and picked you out from the crowd?

4. In your own words, describe what it means to be "desperate" for God.

5. In verse 9 of John 4, in response to Jesus asking her for a drink of water, the Samaritan women reminds Him that she is "unclean." Jesus' response is to ignore her concern over her worldly status because He is more concerned with her eternal status. How would you respond if Jesus ignored all those things you think disqualify you and offered Himself anyway? (Hint: Isn't that what He did on the cross?)

6. Notice in verse 26 of John 4 how the Samaritan woman received the truth of who Jesus was because He saw directly into her heart. He saw her brokenness and her hunger to find that thing that would satisfy her heart. She had not found it in five husbands or her current boyfriend. But when she encountered Jesus and He spoke directly to her heart, she found what she had been looking for all along. She wasn't all "cleaned up" and "fit" for ministry, but her testimony

carried the authority of the One she had encountered. God chose to use her in spite of her brokenness. How has God used you in spite of your brokenness?

GROUP ACTIVATION

Break up into small groups and allow a few minutes for each person to share how they feel they are disqualified and how they would like to be used by God even though they are not "qualified." (At this point, hopefully everyone feels very "safe" in their small groups.) Invite everyone to be as open and honest as they can about their disqualifications *and* how they would like to be used by God. Once everyone has had a few moments to share, go around the group and take time to pray for each person, asking God to respond to the deep desires of that person's heart to be used by Him (God).

PRAYER

O, Father, You knew each one of us before the foundations of the world, before we were formed in our mother's womb. You have loved us with an everlasting love through Your Son, Jesus Christ. Take us now, with our imperfections and failings, and make us into Your new wineskins. We are lost without You, desperate for You. We cannot accomplish Your will outside of Your power and authority. You are our heart's true home, the One we have been longing for. Pick us out of the crowd. Hear our cries—"Take me, pick me! Choose me! Use me!" You are the pearl of great price and we will go anywhere, do anything for You. Amen.

SESSION NOTES

NEW WINESKINS

No one sews a patch of unshrunk cloth on an old garment, for the patch will pull away from the garment, making the tear worse. Neither do men pour new wine into old wineskins. If they do, the skins will burst, the wine will run out and the wineskins will be ruined. No, they pour new wine into new wineskins, and both are preserved (Matthew 9:16-17).

In this analogy, Jesus is explaining that He brings a newness that old containers cannot contain. When Jesus comes into our life, we must put off the old and put on the new. We must become a new, "born again" creation. We have to let go (pour out) the old, stale wine and receive the new wine that Jesus brings into our "cleaned up" selves. In verse 28 of John 4, the Samaritan woman, upon realizing that she has encountered the Messiah, the living water, leaves her water jar and goes back to her village. She has left behind that which she doesn't need because she has something better—she has "living water" to take back to her village.

When we encounter Jesus, if we will receive Him we will no longer have a need for our old habits and behaviors and thought patterns that took us away from God. Jesus will supply all our needs. In Him, we will find everything we have been looking for.

REFLECTION

1. What is God calling you to leave behind now that you have encountered His matchless Son?

2. Why is it sometimes hard to leave those old things of the world behind?

3. What do you see Jesus offering you that is better than the things you cling to?

PRAYER DIRECTIVE

Take Psalm 139 and pray through it now, asking God to take anything that is offensive in you and remove it and to lead you in His ways, always.

O Lord, you have searched me and you know me. You know when I sit and when I rise; you perceive my thoughts from afar. You discern my going out and my lying down; you are familiar with all my ways. Before a word is on my tongue you know it completely, O Lord. You hem me in—behind and before; you have laid your hand upon me. Such knowledge is too wonderful for me, too lofty for me to attain.

Where can I go from your Spirit? Where can I flee from your presence? If I go up to the heavens, you are there; if I make my bed in the depths, you are there. If I rise on the wings of the dawn, if I settle on the far side of the sea, even there your hand will guide me, your right hand will hold me fast.

If I say, "Surely the darkness will hide me and the light become night around me," even the darkness will not be dark to you; the night will shine like the day, for darkness is as light to you. For you created my inmost being; you knit me together in my mother's womb. I praise you because I am fearfully and wonderfully made; your works are wonderful, I know that full well.

My frame was not hidden from you when I was made in the secret place. When I was woven together in the depths of the earth, your eyes saw my unformed body. All the days ordained for me were written in your book before one of them came to be.

How precious to me are your thoughts, O God! How vast is the sum of them! Were I to count them, they would outnumber the grains of sand. When I awake, I am still with you.

…Search me, O God, and know my heart; test me and know my anxious thoughts. See if there is any offensive way in me, and lead me in the way everlasting (Psalm 139:1–18, 23-24).

HOW HUNGRY ARE YOU?

"Here comes that dreamer!" they said to each other. "Come now, let's kill him and throw him into one of these cisterns and say that a ferocious animal devoured him. Then we'll see what comes of his dreams" (Genesis 37:19-20).

In the book of Genesis, beginning in Chapter 37 we find the story of Joseph. He has had a dream in which he saw his brothers bowing down to him. He didn't really understand what it meant, but he shared the dream with his family. His brothers became jealous and threw him into an abandoned well hoping an animal would come along and eat him and they would be rid of him; then they changed their minds and sold him as a slave instead. Thus began many years of trial for Joseph. Through it all, he somehow maintained his integrity and did not abandon God, even when he was given authority in Pharaoh's court. When a great famine came upon the land, God put Joseph in charge and used him to save many, including his (Joseph's) family.

You may or may not endure severe trials in your life, but no matter what your circumstances God wants you to be hungry for Him, for a relationship with Him. Joseph was given a position of power and authority in Pharaoh's court. Everything about Egypt and their culture went against the culture Joseph had been raised in, yet in the midst of the temptations of the world, Joseph was hungry for the things of God. And God saw his heart and used Joseph.

REFLECTIONS AND QUESTIONS

Take time today to read through the story of Joseph in Genesis, reflecting on the many difficulties that Joseph experienced and how God used Joseph.

1. What difficulties are you experiencing or have experienced, and how did you respond in your heart to these challenging times?

2. What has God's response been to what He sees in your heart?

BEYOND OUR FAILURES

*Immediately a rooster crowed. Then Peter remembered the word Jesus
had spoken: "Before the rooster crows, you will disown me three times."
And he went outside and wept bitterly* (**Matthew 26:74-75**).

The disciple Peter experienced failure in trying to follow Jesus. Confused and afraid, he denied his beloved Master before the crucifixion. And this wasn't the only time Peter messed up. He seemed to have a habit of taking action first and thinking later, of speaking first and thinking later. He was a man of action, but not always wise. Most of us can identify with Peter. Our intentions can be good, but sometimes we just mess up.

Peter was so broken inside by his betrayal of Jesus that all he knew to do was to go back and be a fisherman again. After spending three amazing years with the Son of God, Peter messed up and then put his tail between his legs and slunk off hoping to disappear and be forgotten. But God had other plans. He came lovingly to Peter and ministered reconciliation and then sent him out to be used mightily to build His Church.

REFLECTIONS AND QUESTIONS

Read chapter 21 in the book of John, reflecting on the meaning of the word *love* as it is found in verses 15–17. Jesus kept pressing the same question upon Peter because He wanted Peter to realize the true meaning of love—the kind of love in which our entire will, everything in us, is involved. He wanted Peter to understand how the disposition of our heart must be fully toward God in every way. That is what God is looking for. He will look beyond your failures and your weaknesses if your heart is fully His.

1. What will it take for you to fully give your heart to God? What is holding you back?

2. What failures loom so large in your life that you think God could never really use you for anything significant?

3. How has God attempted to reconcile you to Him in light of your failures?

PRAYER DIRECTIVE

Spend time in prayer today, thanking Him for the gift of His Son, Jesus. Acknowledge to Him that you know you are forgiven of your sins. Surrender those things that are keeping you from fully giving your heart to God. Ask Him for a full revelation of His great love for you.

GOD WILL MAKE YOU QUALIFIED

Moses said to the Lord, "O Lord, I have never been eloquent, neither in the past nor since you have spoken to your servant. I am slow of speech and tongue. ...O Lord, please send someone else to do it" (Exodus 4:10, 13).

Moses felt very unqualified for what God was calling him to. He really couldn't understand how he was going to accomplish God's purposes. He felt unfit for the job, and yet God used him anyway. Boy, did God use Moses! It has been said that God doesn't call the qualified; He qualifies the called. You may feel entirely unqualified to serve God in any significant way, but God doesn't see you that way. If He calls you, He will give you what you need to accomplish His purposes. Moses didn't always do everything right, but God kept on working with Him, qualifying him for the tasks ahead.

God wants us to learn to rely on Him every minute. He doesn't tend to give us everything we need in one big package and then stand back while we go at it. He wants a relationship with us—one in which we stay in fellowship with Him all the time. He wants us to learn to hear His voice in all things and to trust Him to provide when we need provision. God's provision includes qualification. He will continue to qualify us as needed. We are never going to feel entirely qualified, entirely ready. We must learn to trust God at all times to provide what we need, when we need it, because He is trustworthy. In this way, He receives all the glory!

REFLECTIONS AND QUESTIONS

Read First Samuel 17, reflecting particularly on verses 32–37. It is easy to understand that in his own strength, David was not qualified to kill Goliath. He was a boy coming up against a mighty fighting man, and a very large one at that. But David understood that God was for him.

He had a history with God. He knew God to be faithful in the past and expected God to come through again. David trusted God enough to risk his life and the honor of God's people, and God didn't let him down. Notice how, in verses 38–40, David takes off the heavy armor that has been placed on him because he wants to use what is familiar to him. He doesn't try to be something he is not; instead he does what he knows best and trusts God for the rest.

1. Why is David's strategy so wise?

2. Think of a time when you tried to be something you are not in order to answer God's call. What were the results?

3. Now, think of a time when you trusted God to "qualify" you for a situation that you felt unqualified for. How did God respond?

PRAYER DIRECTIVE

Father, I thank you that my weakness is made perfect in Your strength. I thank You that You know what I need before the words are even on my lips. I thank You that You are Jehovah-Jireh, the Lord who provides. Grant me courage to trust You in all the trials of life, in all faith believing that You will qualify me to act in Your name with confidence and authority. Amen.

FOR HIS GLORY

When I came to you, brothers, I did not come with eloquence or superior wisdom as I proclaimed to you the testimony about God. For I resolved to know nothing while I was with you except Jesus Christ and him crucified. I came to you in weakness and fear, and with much trembling. My message and my preaching were not with wise and persuasive words, but with a demonstration of the Spirit's power, so that your faith might not rest on men's wisdom, but on God's power (1 Corinthians 2:1–5).

Rolland and Heidi Baker are founders of IRIS Ministries. Many years ago, the Bakers decided that they wanted to find the poorest place on earth and go there as missionaries so that whatever was accomplished through them could only be attributed to God. It was important to them that God receive all the glory. Like the apostle Paul, Heidi and Rolland knew that they were unable to advance the Kingdom in their own strength.

When God called them to Mozambique they went, and there they found one of the poorest places imaginable. In the years since they first arrived, they have again and again faced what seem like insurmountable obstacles, and yet God always provides. They like to say that "there is always enough" as they go about the impossible task of feeding thousands every day. Many days they get up in the morning not knowing where the food will come from, and yet it comes. Sometimes God literally multiplies the food as they are handing it out. Usually the Bakers aren't the ones actually handing it out—it is typically a worker or someone visiting on a short-term mission team who sees the miracle provision of God. Rolland and Heidi love it when God shows up in the most impossible of situations because that is when He can unequivocally receive all the glory.

REFLECTIONS AND QUESTIONS

With the Bakers' story and the verses from First Corinthians 2:1–5 to reflect on, think of any situations in which God showed up in your life in seemingly impossible situations. If this has not yet happened, think of what it would look like in your life if it did.

1. Have you ever had to work to get yourself out of the way so that all you know is Jesus Christ and Him crucified? What happened as a result of your desire to give God all the glory?

2. The life and death of Jesus Christ is the ultimate act of glorifying God. With the knowledge that Christ lives within you in the power of the Holy Spirit, are you ready to begin living a life in complete surrender, trusting God for everything you need?

3. If you are unable to answer *yes*, right now, what is holding you back? Ask God to remove any impediments in your life so that you can step into the life He has for you since before the foundations of the world.

If your answer is a resounding *yes*, then go forth in the power and authority of God, for His glory, until all have heard the good news and been touched by His love!

Then Jesus came to them and said, "All authority in heaven and on earth has been given to me. Therefore go and make disciples of all nations, baptizing them in the name of the Father and of the Son and of the Holy Spirit, and teaching them to obey everything I have commanded you. And surely I am with you always, to the very end of the age" (Matthew 28:18–20).

And this gospel of the kingdom will be preached in the whole world as a testimony to all nations (Matthew 24:14).

ABOUT RANDY CLARK

Randy Clark, with a D.Min. from United Theological Seminary, is the founder of Global Awakening, a teaching, healing, and impartation ministry that crosses denominational lines. An in-demand international speaker, he leads the Apostolic Network of Global Awakening and travels extensively for conferences, international missions, leadership training, and humanitarian aid. Randy and his wife, DeAnne, live in Pennsylvania.

WATCH GOD ACCOMPLISH THE MIRACULOUS

THROUGH YOU.

LEARN FROM DR. RANDY CLARK!

Every Christian has been sent and empowered by Jesus to heal the sick. The problem is that many of us don't know how to practically complete this task.

In the *Power to Heal* curriculum, international evangelist, teacher, and apostolic voice, Dr. Randy Clark, shares eight practical, Bible-based tools that will help you start praying for the sick and see them supernaturally healed!

 Destiny Image is a division of Nori Media Group.

THE HOLY SPIRIT
WANTS TO WORK THROUGH YOU!

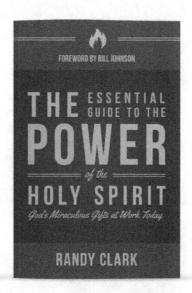

MANY CHRISTIANS HAVE EMBRACED THE DECEPTION THAT THE HOLY SPIRIT IS NO LONGER AT WORK.

But Dr. Randy Clark, President and Founder of Global Awakening, has been an *eyewitness* to the miraculous work of the Holy Spirit and a *key participant* in watching Him powerfully transform lives throughout the world. In this easy-to-read guide, he equips believers to understand and walk in the power of the Spirit every day.

• Discover the gifts of the Holy Spirit that are available to you.

• Recognize an authentic move of God in your church, community, & life.

• Understand how miracles, signs, and wonders play a key role evangelism.

FULFILL YOUR DESTINY! UNLOCK THE POWER OF THE HOLY SPIRIT IN YOUR LIFE.

 Destiny Image is a division of Nori Media Group.

Christian Prophetic
CERTIFICATION PROGRAM

We are happy to announce the launch of the
**Christian Prophetic Certification Program
(CPCP).**

CPCP will teach students how to recognize the gift of prophecy in their own life, allowing them to better recognize communications from the Holy Spirit.

Students will gain a truly Biblical perspective on the prophetic both from the Old and New Testaments. They will also learn about the history of prophesy within the church, its benefits and the ways in which it went off track.

**Courses are available online
and can be taken anywhere at any time.**

Check out our website for more details at
propheticcertification.com

JOIN US!

globalawakening

lighting fires • building bridges • casting vision

Based in Mechanicsburg, PA, the Apostolic Network of Global Awakening (ANGA) is a teaching, healing and impartation ministry with a heart for the nations. Founded in 1994 by Randy Clark after his involvement with the Toronto Airport Christian Fellowship revival, the ministry exists to fulfill the biblical commissions of Jesus:

> *As you go preach, saying the Kingdom of heaven is at hand. Heal the sick, cleanse the lepers, raise the dead, cast out demons. Freely you have received, freely give (Matthew 10:7-8).*

> *Therefore go and make disciples of all nations, baptizing them in the name of the Father and of the Son and of the Holy Spirit, and teaching them to obey everything I have commanded you. And surely I am with you always, to the very end of the age (Matthew 28:19-20).*

Through the formation of ANGA, International Ministry Trips (IMT), the Schools of Healing and Impartation and the Global School of Supernatural Ministry, Global Awakening offers training, conferences, humanitarian aid, and ministry trips in an effort to raise up a company of men and women who will facilitate revival among the nation's leaders. By providing an assortment of international training opportunities, the ministry works in accordance with the revelation to the Apostle Paul regarding the purpose of the five fold ministries:

> *It was He who gave some to be apostles, some to be prophets, some to be evangelists, and some to be pastors and teachers, to prepare God's people for works of service, so that the body of Christ may be built up until we all reach unity in the faith and in the knowledge of the Son of God and become mature, attaining to the whole measure of the fullness of Christ (Ephesians 4:11-13).*

Led by Rev. Randy Clark, the ministry has visited over 36 countries and continues to travel extensively to bring hope, healing, and power to the nations.

globalawakening.com

Made in United States
Orlando, FL
14 March 2023